What Am I Supposed to Do NOW?!?

Coping With Teen Grief

Juanita Walters

Table of Contents

Introduction

I know you must be feeling really sad right now. Sometimes life deals us really tough blows like losing someone extremely special to us. It could be a family member you loved dearly or a close friend you told everything to and cared for deeply. No matter what exact situation brings you to this book, I want you to know that I understand how upsetting it can feel. Your heart likely aches and it may seem like the sadness will never go away. Just take it from me; grieving is really difficult to deal with.

Losing someone you really cared about can turn your whole world upside down. One moment they're right there with you and then suddenly they're gone. It's almost like a part of you disappeared too, leaving this enormous and really painful hollow feeling inside. You begin to feel really sad, empty, or lonely all the time now. The little things that used to make you smile might just make you burst into tears instead. It's so hard because one second you can be okay, and the next second everything hits you at once and you completely lose it.

Please don't be too hard on yourself; it is completely normal to feel all over the place when you're grieving. Our body and mind go through a whole process to help us deal with and accept what happened. Grief is natural, but I know that as a teen, it can be really overwhelming and confusing too. You're likely thinking things like, *Why does this hurt so much? When will the pain go away?* and *What am I supposed to do now?*

The reason I created this book is to help you understand that you aren't alone in dealing with these painful emotions and to provide some strategies for getting through each day. Most of all, I want you to remember that everything you've been feeling is completely normal. Grief is a natural human response when we lose someone or something special in our lives. It's totally okay for you to feel sad, mad, lonely, or any other way as you go through this.

As human beings, we form deep attachments to the people and pets in our lives. When they die or go away, our brains actually go through withdrawal from the loss of that attachment and relationship. That's what causes the physical and emotional pain of grief. Our bodies and minds need time to process and make sense of what happened so we can start to heal. It's all part of the grieving process.

Healing from this loss won't happen overnight. It can often take weeks, months, or even years to work through everything you've gone through. Be patient with your emotions as you go through such a tough journey. Allow yourself to feel whatever comes up, whether it's sadness, anger, or anything else, without putting yourself down. Talking to close friends and family who care about you can help a lot. There's no single right or wrong way to grieve; every person grieves differently based on their unique experiences and feelings. Don't compare how you're coping to others—you're doing the best you can. And even if some days it's really hard, continue being gentle with yourself like you would if a good friend needs you.

The most important thing is that you take care of yourself. Eat healthy meals when you can stomach food. Get some exercise, even if it's just going for walks. Try to maintain good sleep routines. Find relaxing activities that give you a break from grieving, even if it's just listening to music or watching silly videos for a little while each day. It's also key to let out your feelings in a safe way, whether through journaling, talking to therapists or support groups, making art or music, and more. Bottling everything up will only make things harder.

I know you probably feel alone in your grief right now. But I want you to know that you aren't alone in experiencing this kind of pain. Almost everybody will experience loss at some point in their lives. At your age, chances are many of your friends have gone through grief too, whether they experienced a death in their family, a friend, or a pet. Some may even be dealing with it at the same time as you. Try connecting with your peers; you'd be surprised at how much comfort there can be in realizing you're not alone. I've also included suggestions later in this book for finding grief support groups near you that are full of others your age who "get it."

As for what to expect in the grieving process, it's a rollercoaster for sure. You'll have good and bad moments each day or even each hour. Some days will seem unbearable, while others will allow you to feel more like yourself again temporarily before another wave hits. Over time, though, the low moments won't come as often or be as intensely painful. Memories will become easier to look back on instead of sharp knives in your heart. You'll start to find a new sense of normal without the person or pet you've lost.

One important thing I want to assure you of is that grieving doesn't make you weak or crazy. It's a sign of how much you care! Caring means that losses can really, really hurt. But over time, that hurt will soften into more of an ache as scars form in the shape of beautiful memories. Your loved one or pet may no longer be with you physically, but the love lives on in your heart and the lessons they taught you. Eventually, your happy memories will outweigh the pain of their loss. The day will come when you can think of them and smile through your tears instead of crying with your whole body. But getting there takes courage, time, and patience.

Some key things to remember about healing from grief are:

- There is no set timetable; each person heals at their own pace, so don't compare yourself to others.

- It's okay and normal to feel physical pain like tightness in your chest, stomach aches, headaches, exhaustion, and more. Grief affects the body and soul.

- Bad days will come less often, but small reminders may still hurt for a long time.

- Mourn however you need to; don't let anyone tell you how to feel or for how long.

- Your emotions may surprise you; let them out safely through journaling, art, and talking. Don't shut down.

- Avoid making big life changes too quickly while grieving; your judgment isn't the best at this time.

- Reach out for support; talking helps you process your emotions and prevents you from isolating yourself.

- Be patient and gentle with yourself like you would a hurting friend.

- Appreciate small moments of joy when they come; grief comes in waves.

- Keep traditions or routines that make you feel close to your loved one.

I'm here for you every step of the way as you walk this path, either through this book or by finding local resources. This book will give you suggestions on coping day by day, ways to honor and remember loved ones, how to handle anniversary dates and holidays, advice for dealing with tough emotions, and lots more. You've got this. Grief takes courage and strength, and you have both. I hope the coming pages offer you tools, comfort, and hope whenever you need them. But for now, know that what you feel is normal and you don't have to walk this road alone. This too shall pass in time, even if it doesn't always feel that way.

I don't know your specific situation or who you've lost, but from one human being to another, I want you to hear that I'm so sorry for your pain. Your feelings are valid and I see you. I know how hard this is, but I also promise there will come a day when the beauty of your memories outweighs the confusion and agony of loss. For now, be gentle with yourself, find strength in others when possible, and keep going one moment at a time. The light ahead is worth walking toward, even if you can't see it yet. We're all here with you on the journey.

Chapter 1:

Riding the Emotional

Roller Coaster

By now, you've started this book because you're feeling all kinds of big emotions after losing someone close. It totally makes sense—grief is one intense roller coaster ride for sure. One thing I bet you're feeling a lot of is confusion over why this happened and why it had to be you. Like, what did you even do to deserve to feel this way? Why did they have to be the ones to leave you behind? All these "Why me?" questions are totally natural when we're grieving. But unfortunately, there usually isn't a clear answer that makes total sense. Sometimes bad things just happen without any explanation. I know that doesn't make it any less painful, though.

All you can do is accept that life is unfair sometimes, even if it doesn't seem fair now that you're the one left hurting. I promise that in time, focusing less on the "why" and more on cherishing your memories will help. You'll learn to find meaning in how much they meant to you rather than why they couldn't have stayed longer. But for now, let those confused and angry "Why?!" feelings out—they're part of the grieving process.

You may find your emotions surprising as you adjust to your loss. One minute you'll think you're doing okay, and then bam—out of nowhere, something will trigger a wave of fresh pain. It could be seeing a photo, hearing a song, or passing their favorite spot. Tiny reminders have a way of sneaking up on us. Don't be hard on yourself when this happens. Grief has no timetable or schedule; it comes and goes unexpectedly.

Crying is actually really healthy for releasing tension, so if tears start falling, go with it. Resisting or bottling up your feelings will only make them stronger later on. Let the tears flow until you can't cry anymore; you'll likely feel at least a tiny bit better having fully felt that moment of grief. And it's okay to not feel okay. Grief hurts so don't apologize for being sad or let anyone tell you how long is too long to mourn.

You know in movies how people always yell at the sky or rain and just let everything out when they're mourning someone? Well, that release of anguish is actually pretty accurate to real-life grieving. You might find yourself screaming, raging, or sobbing uncontrollably at times. Don't censor your natural human reactions—holler, punch pillows, write angry letters you'll never send. Whatever helps you process those overwhelming surges of grief is okay. Just do it safely and with trusted support, if possible.

On the flip side, in between waves of intense sadness, you might feel almost numb or in a daze. This is your mind's way of giving you a break from intense pain. Don't worry—you're not getting over it or moving on yet. Numbness and detachment are simply other healthy defense mechanisms our brains use to cope when the barrage of emotions would be too much otherwise. If it's been your main state for too long, though, it may mean you need to actively grieve more to process what happened. But short periods of detachment are normal too.

Speaking of getting over it, let me be clear: grief isn't something you just get over. It's a process that evolves and changes shape over time as you heal. Those waves of intense emotion might become less frequent as time passes, but you'll likely always feel their loss to some degree. Holidays, milestones, and anniversaries may always sting a bit. And that's okay—it's a sign of how deeply you cared. As long as the pain becomes more of a gentle ache than a fresh wound, you're making progress.

Don't put pressure on yourself to feel certain emotions by certain dates either. There is no expiration date on grief. Some people say it's a year, but everyone grieves differently. Go at your own, healthy pace. Listen to yourself; whenever you start feeling like participating in life again without raw agony, this is the right time for you. But accept that you may always carry a loving scar shaped by your memories too.

Try to go with the flow; when sadness hits, feel it fully. When numbness comes, accept the reprieve. And don't judge your emotional journey—grief is never the same for anyone. Be gentle with yourself through this intensely rocky time. Talk through your feelings whenever you need reassurance that you're not crazy or alone in whatever you're experiencing. With patience and self-care, I promise this roller coaster ride of a process will gradually smooth out over time. But for now, hang on tight, even through the turbulent parts.

It's okay to not feel okay—that in itself is part of getting through grief in a healthy way. So, please don't bottle up your complex emotions or apologize for them. Let them out safely through the activities and trusted people around you whenever waves hit.

Write in this book whenever you need to get your feelings down privately as you ride the roller coaster. Send angry letters to the sky that no one else will see. Rage, scream, sob—then come back here to look at happy photos and remind yourself of brighter memories too. With support, honesty, and balance, each intense wave of grief will run its course before the next one comes. And in between, even brief moments of feeling okay again will start to feel more frequent.

9

You've got incredible strength and heart. I know this journey will try them sorely at times, but you can get through anything with courage, patience, and allowing yourself to truly feel it all. Take a deep breath; this too shall pass, even on days when it doesn't feel that way. Take care of yourself and keep going, one moment at a time.

Feeling All the Feels: Understanding Your Emotions

Dealing with grief is tough enough without feeling like your emotions are going totally haywire. I remember when my grandpa passed away, I went through what felt like every feeling in the book—anger, sadness, fear, guilt, relief—you name it, I felt it. It was super confusing and made me think maybe I was losing my mind a little! But the truth is, wild emotions are actually really normal when you're grieving.

Our feelings help us process loss and heal over time. Recognizing what you're feeling is half the battle because then you'll know it's not just you; it's all part of the grieving process. Knowing that can help take some of the pressure off.

Anger

Anger is a huge one that a lot of us feel. And it makes total sense—someone was taken from you against your will, so, of course, it's natural to feel mad! You may find yourself thinking angry thoughts like, *If one more person tells me it'll be okay, I'm going to lose it!* or *I'm so mad, I could punch a wall!* It's okay to admit you feel that way. Anger comes from the pain of loss, so let it fuel you to get through each day instead of bottling it up. Find safe ways to express it, like strenuous exercise, journaling, or the creative arts.

You might also feel angry at the person who passed away. Thoughts like, *I can't believe they left me here alone!* or *Why did they have to get sick, hurt, or die and ruin everything??* are super common too because we feel betrayed by their absence. Know that it doesn't mean you loved them any less; it's normal to feel betrayed by death, even if they didn't cause it on purpose. Let those frustrated feelings flow instead of holding them in.

Hurt

Hurt is another big one after a loss. You might have thoughts like, *My feelings are so hurt, I wasn't ready for them to go yet,* or *Why does this hurt so badly?? Make it stop!*" When we love someone and then lose them, it feels like a heavy emotional blow. Let yourself acknowledge how deeply it wounded your heart. Talk to trusted people about the ache if you need extra comfort during raw moments.

Sadness and Depression

Sadness and depression are obvious but brutal companions to grief. You might relate to thinking, *I just want to sleep all day and forget about everything* or *Being awake hurts too much. I feel so alone.* Those are totally normal reactions to how overwhelming sorrow can feel. Don't try to fight the sadness; feel it fully and it will pass more easily with time. Connecting to others who understand depression may help during low periods.

Fear

Fear can rear its head after loss in numerous ways, like worrying about *What if I forget what their voice or laugh sounded like?* or panicking over missing out on future memories you'll never get to share. Fearing the unknown is our body's natural response to change—even change we don't want. Acknowledge that those scared feelings are simply your loved one's absence filling you with uncertainty. Talking with others may reassure you.

Guilt

Guilt commonly strikes grieving people, bringing thoughts like, *I should have spent more time with them* or *If only I'd called when they were sick.* Try to be gentle; hindsight is always 20/20, and they wouldn't want you suffering now. The past can't change. Express regret over real mistakes while forgiving normal human faults. Focus on making future days full of love.

Relief

Relief is also perfectly normal to feel sometimes amid grief's heaviness. You might think, *At least their suffering is over now* or *Now I don't have to watch them get more ill.* That shows how much you cared; they weren't hurting anymore. Simply put, you're empathizing with what they went through while still missing them enormously. Mixed feelings are okay.

Denial

Denial can feel like constant thoughts of *This can't be real. They have to come back.* or *If I don't think about it, maybe it isn't true.* Our minds try to protect us in early grief by rejecting the loss. That's valid. When you're ready, open your heart to accepting reality while still honoring your relationship. Saying goodbye involves faith that they live on in your heart.

The emotions I mentioned are truly just the tip of the iceberg when it comes to grieving. You may feel happy one moment then cry hysterically or zone out completely. Every feeling is welcome and part of processing what happened in your own time and way. Rather than chasing an elusive normal, accept all your feelings as messengers helping you heal. Listen to them and let them out safely, and gradually, they will teach you to live lovingly with loss.

Something else that makes grief so confusing emotionally is that you might not even realize certain feelings are cropping up inside at first! For example, I didn't consciously know I felt regret or relief until I reflected on my experience much later. Additionally, I would experience anger that would bubble up out of nowhere through tears of sadness. All of that is natural, too. So, be patient with yourself and how complex your feelings are. Don't force labels; just allow whatever comes up to pass through.

With support, your road through all these raw emotions will gradually become less like a potholed dirt road and more like a gentle, winding path over time. The pain lessens as memories grow fonder. Laughs start coming more easily between quiet tears. And instead of demanding you get over it, compassionate loved ones rejoice when they see you smiling again as a reminder of happy times. You will get through this jagged time. For now, be gentle with yourself through the roughest patches. Remember, it's okay and normal to feel any way through this personal journey of healing.

The Roller Coaster of Grief: Ups, Downs, and Loop-the-Loops

By now, you probably know grief is one wild roller coaster ride, huh? One minute you'll feel okay, then all of a sudden, a trigger like a smell or song hits you and the crying starts all over again. It's like your emotions are doing 360° spins, loop-the-loops, and dropping faster than the biggest roller coasters out there!

What's important to know is that this roller coaster is totally normal and part of the grieving process. No one can tell you how or when to feel; your emotions will have their ups and downs whenever they need to. Trying to rush through or control your feelings will just make the ride feel longer. So, let me help you prepare for what to expect with the ebb and flow of grief over time.

First off, grief does have stages. But remember, they aren't linear; you'll likely bounce between them in no particular order as each stage comes and goes. They also don't have set time limits so go at your own pace. The main stages are:

- **Shock and denial:** Feeling disbelief or numb at first, maybe saying things like, "This can't be real" or pretending they're still alive.

- **Pain and guilt:** When it sinks in that they're truly gone, you start to feel intense sadness, anger, regret, and more, and ruminate on what-ifs.

- **Bargaining:** Trying to postpone grieving by thinking *If only...* or *If I could have...* even though it's not logical.

- **Depression:** Deep and prolonged feelings of sadness, grief, despair, crying spells, or losing interest in things

- **Testing and adjusting:** Starting to accept the loss but having waves of intense grief when emerging from the deep pain.

- **Beginning to accept and adapt:** Learning to live with your loss and grieving in more intermittent, less intense ways over time. Memories bring smiles as well as tears now.

Knowing these phases exist can reassure you that whatever you feel is normal—you're not alone or going crazy. Understand that it'll take time to move through them at your own individual pace. There's no set finish line.

One huge thing to prepare for is triggers—the unexpected situations that can cause a sudden wave of emotion out of nowhere. Like sniffing their favorite candle, hearing a song you used to sing together, eating their homemade dish, or noticing their empty chair, triggers will likely hit you for a long time until the pain safely transforms into comfort from cherished memories.

Prepare yourself for how intensely raw triggers can make you instantly sad. At the same time, know that it won't last forever. Crying when you need to lets the pain flow out so you can keep loving your memories without drowning. With each wave, you'll get a little stronger again. Some things to try when hit with triggers are:

- Breathe deeply through your gut until it passes.

- Journal about the memory so it doesn't stay bottled inside.

- Call a friend who understands and talk through it safely.

- Do something relaxing, like art or music, to redirect your thoughts.

- Remind yourself that it's normal to feel this way.

- Remember, they aren't truly gone as long as you hold them in your heart.

Speaking of waves, expect the intensity to fluctuate a lot at first, like a rocky ocean. Some days, life will feel meaningless, while others will have you feeling temporarily distant from the sadness so you can recharge. As sad as the lows are, ride them out; they'll start to feel less bottomless over time. Focus on just getting through each moment, hour, or day. Don't panic, thinking it'll never end. This too shall pass.

After intense periods, take care of yourself with things like cozy self-care, comfort food in moderation, funny movies, or distracting hobbies, if just for a little while. Don't turn to unsafe coping mechanisms like drugs or alcohol; they only delay healthy grieving. Expressing emotions is better than numbing them away.

Allow yourself little comforts, even if there's guilt for not feeling sad enough. You need the energy to face each wave when it comes again. With time, the waves will gradually become gentler and less frequent. Though never fully going away, the grief transforms into you being able to lovingly honor them without pain overwhelming your life.

Remember that grief is complex; you may hop between many emotions, like anger, laughter, crying, and zoning out, all in one day. Be patient with yourself through it. You don't have to understand it or like how raw it feels; just keep choosing self-care daily however you personally need it most. The most important thing is that you feel your feelings as safely as you can.

If grief's hold on you starts scaring you with thoughts like *How can I go on if they aren't here?* then reach for extra support. Leaning on others, whether friends, family, or counseling, shows true strength. No one expects you to be over it already. They just want to be by your side to help carry you through the scary ups and downs.

With each wave coming and going, take courage; you are getting stronger and you do have the inner power to face another day. The intense low points become less bottomless over time and gentle high moments grow more frequent. And one day, reflecting on memories brings a smile before the tears. You've got this—just keep riding the waves, one at a time. This roller coaster will start feeling smoother. You've got an incredible heart to make it through.

It's Okay to be Not Okay: Normalizing Your Feelings

Going through grief sometimes makes you feel like you're totally losing it, doesn't it? Your emotions are all over the place; you can't stop crying and nothing seems to make you happy. It's easy to think there must be something wrong with you for feeling so not okay. But I want you to know that those ups and downs are a completely normal part of grieving. It's okay to not feel okay right now.

Grief is an extremely difficult thing to go through, and it's going to take you on an emotional roller coaster ride, whether you're ready for it or not. Experiencing intense sadness, anger, and confusion are your natural human response to losing someone important. It would be weird not to feel them strongly after a big loss! So, let's talk about why it's normal and healthy to go through what you're going through.

First off, grief is a natural process we all have to experience at some point when we lose someone close to us. It's our innate way of adjusting to change we didn't choose and making sense of intense feelings of loss. Experiencing grief shows how much you cared about the person who died, and it proves you're a compassionate human with a big heart. There's nothing wrong with you for fully feeling your emotions; it shows how much love you have to give.

The ups and downs are also totally normal. Some days you might feel okay, only to completely break down and cry later. Or you could bounce between angry and sad quickly. Unexpected triggers can make you grieve all over again too. Sudden switches between feelings are your mind and body's natural way of coping with intense sorrow.

It's also very normal to feel confused, scared, or even guilty while grieving. Death can turn your world upside down. Thoughts like *I should be over this by now* or *I don't know how to keep going* are common but totally understandable human reactions as you adjust. Having mixed feelings of sadness, relief, and anger at once is too. Grief isn't simple or straightforward. Be gentle with yourself as your emotions figure things out in a healthy way.

Sometimes grieving may even cause physical symptoms like stomach aches, headaches, no appetite, or exhaustion. This grief sickness occurs because stress affects your body as much as your mind and heart. Let yourself rest if your grief feels overwhelming, and know that these reactions are valid too. Give your body what it needs to nurture strength for hard days.

One of the biggest things to realize is that there's no normal timeline for grief. Some people cry for weeks or months, while others may smile more quickly, but both are healthy responses based on different personalities and individual experiences of loss. The most important thing is to go at your own pace, in a caring way, through this journey.

Whether your feelings are intense, occasional, or you feel nothing at all, it's okay. Some grievers bottle up feelings for long periods and then break down. For others, the opposite happens. There's no wrong way as long as you're not harming yourself or punishing yourself for how you're coping. Have grace for wherever you are in the process each day.

Remind yourself often that these ups and downs of emotions, confusion, and self-doubt are healthy and natural responses. Some days will be better, some worse—all equally valid parts of healing. Treat yourself with kindness like you would a hurting friend.

With patience and self-care over time, your journey will find more calm waters between the rough seas. But till then, keep bravely choosing to care for yourself through the tears. You deserve comfort, and allowing whatever you feel to pass shows such courage and strength of character. Give your heart permission to grieve fully in whatever way feels right. There's nothing wrong with not feeling okay. You're doing amazing.

Making It Real

Megan's story is a good example of how grief doesn't always look the same for everyone. When she was just four years old, her mom died suddenly in a terrible car accident. Megan still has bits of foggy memories from back then—seeing flashing lights, crying a lot, and lots of unfamiliar faces. But because she was so young, she didn't fully comprehend what had really happened.

Her aunt Susan and uncle Tim quickly took her in to raise as their own child. They loved Megan dearly and did their absolute best to give her a happy home filled with support and stability. But the reality was, Megan's mom had been ripped away from her life in an instant, and as much as her new family tried to keep her from feeling the full blow of sorrow, deep down she was still deeply grieving, even if she didn't understand it herself.

As Megan grew older, her unprocessed grief started coming out little by little in unhealthy ways that confused her. She'd get super angry or upset for no clear reason, sometimes taking it out verbally on family and friends who only wanted to help. Her schoolwork and behavior slipped as she lost interest in daily activities. Megan often just wanted to be alone instead of socializing too.

Her loved ones were worried and tried talking to her, but Megan insisted she was fine and didn't know what was wrong either. On the inside, she felt helpless and ashamed of her erratic emotions, swinging from explosive anger to numb detachment. It made her start to believe something must be deeply wrong with her as a person.

The grieving toll really began catching up to Megan in middle school. Her grades plunged more than ever, and she got suspended twice for fighting at school after losing control over tiny triggers. Home life became strained too as she continuously butted heads with everyone and was isolated in her room. Her aunt and uncle were at their wit's end and out of concern, finally insisted on counseling.

That's when Megan's suppressed childhood grief finally began to emerge, bit by bit. With gentle encouragement, Megan started opening up about her hazy memories of flashing lights and sirens and being shuffled around between unfamiliar faces crying for her mommy after the accident. She talked about feeling like an outsider living with an adopted family even though they loved her endlessly.

As Megan spoke more, she began connecting the dots between the loss of her mother at age four and the unstable emotions that had been quietly destroying parts of her life for years without understanding why. Saying it all out loud for the first time brought a strong wave of painful feelings that Megan had kept buried deep inside herself for over a decade. It hit her that she'd been grieving the whole time without realizing it.

From then on, Megan really took therapy seriously as a safe space to process childhood memories, ask adult questions about death she never got answers to before, and embrace the complex emotions gradually rising up inside her to heal from suppressed grief. She learned to accept the intense sadness, confusion, anger, and longing she still felt for her mom after losing her so young without warning or explanation.

Having those realizations, Megan let herself forgive herself at last for reactions and behavior that came from the buried sorrow she didn't know how to handle or name for so long. She learned healthy coping mechanisms and made efforts to strengthen supportive relationships with family again through open communication. Things didn't magically get easy overnight, but she found a new sense of liberation and understanding in herself.

Now Megan wants to share her story to help others know that grief doesn't look the same for everyone and it's never too late to process feelings that have been bottled up inside without recognition for years. She's come a long way from being that angry, depressed middle schooler and has found inner peace through honest introspection. Her message these days is simple: It's okay to not feel okay, and getting real help is so important to healing in your own time.

Megan's experience proves how easily children can suppress or compartmentalize deep grief instinctively without a conscious understanding of exactly what they're feeling or why. But the heaviness doesn't just go away on its own; it stays trapped, waiting to emerge sometime later in unhealthy ways if left unaddressed. With compassion and the willingness to reflect, even old wounds and confusing shadows can find light again, given time and guidance. Her story reminds us to nurture open communication through sensitive changes.

Most of all, Megan wants others not to feel ashamed like she once did for human reactions to unexplainable losses we don't choose. Having her own "aha!" moment of clarity proved even the longest buried sorrow can transform into strength through honest tears once their source is named. Her resilience after so much suppressed inner turmoil serves as powerful inspiration—it's never too late to begin your healing journey and no journey is too huge to start making steps forward if done with patience and care for ourselves. We all walk our personal roads at our own pace.

So, whether grief hits you young like Megan or as a teen, never feel afraid to get real help from counseling if upsetting emotions have you confused or you don't feel okay. There's no limit on time or age to better understand our own hearts. With compassion and willingness, even the darkest shadows find light in their own time through our resilient human capacity to love and support ourselves and our ability to keep bravely going each new day despite life's unfair losses. Megan's story is one of quiet courage in that spirit.

What Am I Supposed to Do Now?

Small steps of self-care every day, acknowledging your emotions, learning about triggers, and practicing mindfulness are proven ways grievers have found peace gradually through the chaos. So, take a deep breath. You've got this, even if it doesn't always feel that way. One moment at a time, okay?

First and most important is acknowledging how you truly feel inside instead of bottling up emotions. Share your deepest thoughts and memories with someone you trust completely, whether a close friend, family member, teacher, counselor, or spiritual advisor. It's so healing to have compassionate ears to listen without judgment as you verbalize your pain, questions, anger, and longing out loud. Keep communicating through your ups and downs for comfort.

Talking lets feelings flow out so your heart has space to keep loving memories of your person without drowning in grief alone. It's not about being fine or getting over it; it's about honoring your journey, however raw it feels, through honesty. Journaling privately can also help capture thoughts and feelings when talking aloud isn't an option in the moment.

Something else to be aware of is your personal triggers—situations that come out of nowhere to reignite sadness unexpectedly. For some, it may be smells, tastes, holidays, locations, photos, or songs closely tied to special shared memories. When hit by triggers, breathe deeply and accept whatever you need to feel as it passes. As time goes on, triggers hurt less and start enhancing the treasured memories behind them.

It's also healthy to acknowledge painful realities you may resist facing. Saying aloud something like "My dad is really gone and won't be here for birthdays or holidays anymore" can feel unbearable at first, but verbalizing the unthinkable does help you process and adjust internally over repeated exposures with self-care. Show yourself compassion through even the roughest waves, one day at a time.

Practicing mindfulness during grief involves focusing attention on the present moment rather than dwelling on the past or panicking about what's ahead. Ground yourself through deep breathing, describing five things you see, hear, or feel, or simply appreciating small mercies all around you in nature that continue. When swamped in sadness, mindfulness offers an anchor to reality and respite from dark thoughts.

These little self-care actions add up over time to more peaceful mourning. Be patient on your journey; some days will naturally flow easier than others. When you are extra overwhelmed, it's okay to seclude yourself temporarily to recharge rather than forcing fake okayness. Always choose patience and compassion wherever you are, minute by minute, through this challenging ride.

Each small success along the way, like having an honest cry with support, facing a trigger bravely, or using mindfulness to get through an anguished hour, shapes inner tranquility from the rubble. Staying connected to others and your deeper purpose or spirit also strengthens your healing energy to keep facing a sunnier tomorrow despite the storms today.

One additional thing to remember is that there's no finish line for grief; mourning looks different from day to day and person to person. Be proud of every step forward through your emotions, whether big or small, and don't apologize for how long you need to heal. Self-care helps you honor their memory in a healthy, hopeful way without pain dictating life.

So, whenever doubts start creeping in about how to pick up pieces alone or what you're supposed to be doing now, reflect back gently on your journey and take heart—you've already gotten through more than you realize by leaning on loving support. No day is perfectly okay in grief, but you've proven your resilience by just facing each sunrise, minute by minute. There's nothing wrong as long as you keep choosing life with compassion.

Chapter 2:

The Reality of Loss

Losing someone you care about is one of the hardest things anyone can go through. When it first happens, it can feel absolutely unreal—like you're trapped in some sort of nightmare that you just can't wake up from, no matter how hard you try. Your whole world gets turned upside down in an instant. One minute, that person was there with you—laughing, smiling, texting you goodnight—and the next, they're just...gone. Poof. As if they were never even there to begin with.

I remember when it first happened to me. I came home from school and my mom sat me down on the couch with a look on her face like something terrible had happened. She told me in a shaky voice that my best friend Emily had been in a really bad car accident after volleyball practice and didn't make it. As soon as the words came out of her mouth, it was like my brain just short-circuited. I literally couldn't process what she was saying. It didn't make any sense. Emily was fine that morning when I saw her; we even made plans to meet up after school. This had to be some kind of mistake.

But I knew, by the way my mom was crying, that it wasn't. An icy cold feeling washed over me from head to toe. It felt like my heart had just been ripped right out of my chest. I started shaking uncontrollably and let out this guttural wail like an animal that had been wounded. I stumbled to my room and collapsed onto my bed, clutching one of Emily's hoodies that still smelled like her perfume as I screamed and screamed into my pillow. Emily couldn't be gone. She was my best friend; we had known each other since kindergarten and had been inseparable ever since. We had so many plans for high school, college, and our whole lives ahead of us. We promised we'd always be there for each other, no matter what. And now, just like that, she was ripped away from me forever. It didn't seem real or possible. It was too horrible, terrible, and devastating to comprehend.

And that's the thing about loss—it leaves you breathless. The shock of it hits you like a freight train and literally steals the air from your lungs. You gasp and wheeze, grasping at straws to make sense of something that will never, ever make sense, no matter how many times or ways you try to rationalize it. Nothing can truly prepare you for that feeling of the earth dropping out from under your feet. That sense that your entire world as you know it has ended.

In those first few days and weeks, you go through the motions in a complete daze. You eat and sleep only when others make you because taking care of yourself is the absolute furthest thing from your mind. Small, everyday tasks that used to be effortless now feel insurmountably overwhelming. Getting out of bed, getting dressed, brushing your teeth—it all seems unbearably exhausting. School becomes this battlefield that you drag yourself through each day, not absorbing a single thing yet hoping that somehow it will distract you, if only for minutes at a time, from the constant replay in your head of what happened.

News of the person's death spreads through your community and social circle like wildfire, with everyone whispering about it and looking at you with pity in their eyes. Random acquaintances you barely know come up to hug you and say they're sorry as if their empty condolences can somehow magically undo what's been done. Memorials, funerals, and well-meaning gestures threaten to suffocate you. You want to scream at everyone to just leave you alone, but you're in too much of a fog to muster the energy to say the words.

Late at night is the worst when it all crashes over you anew with an even more intense, gut-wrenching wave of grief. You cling to their memory like a lifeline, replaying each tiny detail you can recall—from their laugh to the way their voice sounded to the inside jokes only the two of you shared—terrified that you'll somehow forget even the smallest thing about them if you don't concentrate hard enough to hold onto it. Forgetting even a single moment feels like losing them all over again.

Time does eventually start to pass, though each day remains excruciatingly painful. But little by little, the haze starts to lift, and a sickening, crushing reality sets in—this is your new normal now. This person you cared so deeply for is permanently gone from your life, and nothing will ever be the same without them. The life you imagined doesn't exist anymore. A brutal reminder that bad things really do happen and life isn't always fair. It's a truth too cruel to truly accept.

Losing someone shatters you in a way that nothing else can. The suffering, loneliness, and longing never fully go away; you just learn, bit by agonizing bit, how to carry it. These feelings you're experiencing are valid, real, and shared by others who understand your pain. With time and support from people who care, you will learn to cope. The tightness in your chest will loosen, even if only slightly. One day, the good memories will start to outweigh the bad again. You'll always miss them, but you'll find a way to keep living, which is what I'm sure they would want for you.

Facing the Unthinkable: Dealing With the Death of a Loved One

Nothing can prepare you for the death of someone you love. It's one of the hardest things a person will ever go through in their life. It can make you feel like your entire world has been turned upside down.

When it first happens, it's common to feel completely overwhelmed with thoughts like *What just happened?* and *Is this real?* Losing someone important to you is such a scary, unnatural thing. No one ever plans on having to say goodbye to someone they care about so much, especially when they're young. Their absence leaves this huge, painful hole that can make it hard to function normally again.

Sometimes, death comes more slowly when a loved one passes away after an illness. You watch them get weaker and fade away over time, which allows you to start grieving while they're still alive. But it doesn't make it any easier to accept when the moment finally comes and they're gone. If anything, it can make the feelings of loss and emptiness even more intense because you've had more time to prepare and dread what's coming.

When someone dies after an illness, it's also common to experience intense feelings of guilt—like you could have or should have done more to save them or spent more quality time with them while you still had the chance. You replay all the little moments and conversations in your head, wishing you could change or add to them. But the truth is, none of us are ever fully ready to say goodbye, no matter how long we have to prepare. Be gentle with yourself—what's done is done and they wouldn't want you tormenting yourself over things outside of your control.

One thing most people dealing with loss can agree on is that the sadness can sometimes feel absolutely crushing. Heavy, endless waves of tears leave your whole body aching and drained. At times, you may feel like the grief is suffocating you and you just want to be alone. That's okay—everyone grieves in their own way and time. There's no right or wrong way to mourn as long as you're taking basic care of yourself. But try not to shut yourself off from support for too long, either. People who care about you want to help carry some of your burden during this difficult time.

It may feel strange or wrong at first, but allow yourself to fully feel whatever emotions come up without judgment. Crying if you need to cry, yelling if you need to yell, reminiscing about happy memories together—your grieving process is personal. Suppressing your natural responses won't make the pain go away faster; it'll only build up inside of you over time. Grief has no timeline, so be gentle and patient with yourself as you learn to live with this new normal.

Make sure you take as much care of yourself as possible. Try to maintain healthy eating habits, even if food has lost its taste for now. Stay hydrated; grief causes a lot of physical as well as emotional drain. Get outside in nature or fresh air when you can stand to be around others. Exercise isn't about working off stress right now; it's about moving your body that's likely felt heavy and tired with grief. Schedule little self-care things you enjoy, like a warm bath or Facetime with a friend, to give yourself small boosts each day. Your physical and mental health will thank you.

If, after some time, you find yourself truly struggling to function or still feeling overwhelmingly sad most days, don't hesitate to reach out to a counselor or grief support group.

Speaking with others who truly understand what you're going through can help you process everything properly and feel less alone. There's no shame in admitting you need extra help coping; losing someone important is one of the hardest things life throws our way. Professional support is there to lighten the load when you feel close to breaking.

As the weeks and months pass, the pain of loss eventually starts to lessen its intensity little by little. The good memories will begin to outweigh the bad ones once more as time allows more distance. Your loved one's presence will feel less like a fresh wound and more like a treasured part of who you are. They'll still be deeply missed every single day, but their love has left an imprint on your heart that can never fade away. You'll learn to find purpose and continue living in a way that honors their memory. It's a long journey forward, but you've got this, even if some days still feel too hard to bear alone. You will make it through.

When Life Changes in an Instant: Coping With Sudden Loss

The unexpected, abrupt nature of losing someone suddenly through an accident or act of violence can feel unbearably cruel. One moment your loved one is living their normal, everyday life, and then, without any warning, they're ripped away from you without a chance for proper goodbyes. It's a trauma that rattles you to your core and leaves your mind reeling with painful what-ifs that will haunt you for years.

When someone dies suddenly, there's no long, drawn-out grieving process like with an illness. You don't get that time to prepare your heart and say all the little things left unsaid. You're left with this massive, gaping hole of resentment that you didn't get enough time together or more chances to make happy memories before it was too late. The shock and disbelief can take a long time to wear off because your brain refuses to accept such a senseless loss.

Not getting closure by saying goodbye properly is one of the hardest parts of a sudden death. It leaves you endlessly replaying your last conversations, imagining all the things you wish you could redo or say now that it's too late. You analyze every little word and action, desperate to change or fix something, even though you know deep down it isn't your fault. The what-ifs become an endless torment.

What if you had been with them? What if you had insisted on driving them somewhere instead of letting them go alone? What if you had chosen a different activity that day so they weren't in the wrong place at the wrong time? It's perfectly normal to feel regret, guilt, and anger over all the uncertainties left behind when someone dies out of nowhere like that. But please try your best not to blame yourself. You had no control over fate or the tragic circumstances that took them from you.

It may feel like you should have been able to protect them or that you somehow failed them. I know that it seems impossible to shut off the voice in your head telling you it's your fault, but you need to be gentle with yourself. These twisted thoughts are just a cruel trick your grief is playing. Your loved one wouldn't want you torturing yourself with endless hypotheticals. They loved you, and their loss was simply not something any of us could have predicted or stopped from happening, no matter how much we wish we could rewind time.

Something else common with sudden loss is feeling hollow, numb, and disconnected from the world, like you're going through the motions of daily tasks on autopilot while inside, everything feels surreal and muted. Your loved one's absence leaves this vacant physical sensation in your chest, and at times, your mind simply refuses to accept their death as a permanent reality. Don't be afraid to cry, scream, or whatever else releases the pent-up emotions; suppressing them will only make it harder to let go later on.

When death is unexpected, many feel cheated out of the time they were supposed to have together. Perhaps major life events like weddings, births, vacations, or simple everyday experiences like holidays and birthdays will now forever have an inescapable lingering sadness attached. It's okay to feel anger that the universe took this person away too soon, shattering all the plans and dreams you had built together. Rage is a natural reaction to immense loss like this.

The grief journey following a sudden loss will likely be turbulent and non-linear as you learn to accept your painful new normal. Make sure to lean on friends and loved ones for comfort and distractions during low moments. When ready, see a therapist familiar with trauma; they can help process intense emotions in a healthy way. Joining a grief support group with others experiencing similar loss may provide solace in shared understanding. With time and care for your emotional well-being, the initial shock will soften into a bearable hurt that gets a little easier to carry each day.

Remember that there is light ahead, even if it's impossible to envision now while still drowning in sorrow's depths. Your person lives on wherever you keep their memory—through pictures, favorite songs, and heartfelt stories of who they were. Find ways to honor their spirit as you pick up the pieces. Let their continual love shine through the dark clouds and guide your steps moving forward. Though nothing takes the sting away completely, it brings them closer to transforming grief's heaviness into gold through lived lessons of life's fragility and the need to cherish each moment with loved ones. Stay strong, keep their light close, and walk the difficult road of recovering and reorganizing life after a loss again, one step at a time.

Saying Goodbye: Understanding the Finality of Death

Unfortunately, there are some situations where not having the chance to say goodbye in person leaves you wishing circumstances could have been different. Whether it's an unexpected loss where things happened too suddenly or if the death occurred somewhere far away making visitation impractical, not getting closure through a final farewell can be hard to cope with and leave lingering regret.

However, as difficult as it is, try not to let those feelings of what-if consume you over what was ultimately outside of your control. Focus instead on the loving connection you did share with that person while they were alive. Death is always difficult to face, but concentrating on creating good memories from their life is better for your healing than endlessly wondering about hypothetical scenarios.

Remember that no matter the physical distance or abruptness of their passing, the bond between you exists far beyond earthly limitations. The support, guidance, lessons, and laughs that make up your history together are carried eternally in both your hearts. Their unique spirit lives on within the marks they left on your soul during your time together.

When someone passes, it's normal to grieve what will never come again, like future conversations or milestones that will now only exist in your imagination. However, don't forget that death itself is simply a natural transition; it does not undo or diminish the deep connection cultivated between souls during a lifetime of caring for one another. What truly matters most is not how or when the physical wrapping fades, but rather the imprint left on your internal world through acts of love.

You may find comfort in focusing on memories as a way to still feel close to your loved one despite their earthly absence. Recall your favorite shared experiences together, like inside jokes only the two of you understood and passionate conversations that expanded your mind. Visualizing cherished moments is a beautiful way to bring them back to your heart and mind, if only temporarily, even after physical visitation becomes impossible.

Try keeping a special journal just for jotting down treasured recollections whenever they return to your thoughts. Write in detail about the event itself, including sights, conversation snippets, and your feelings at the time. Hearing your loved one's laugh may become fuzzier over the years, but keeping memories anchored to paper helps prevent their gradual fading. Revisiting fond memories is a meaningful way to feel comforted by their company again and keep the past alive.

If you're close with others affected by the same loss, coming together with photos, mementos, or other keepsakes that spark remembrance can forge strength through shared smiles over tales of your person. Honoring them together by celebrating aspects you admired, like a passion or favorite holiday, reinforces a continuing bond across the divide between living and deceased. Even something simple, like cooking their best-loved recipe, keeps their spirit integrated into life's moments.

Though it may offer little solace now, with time, the stabbing pain of grief does gradually soften into a scar that remains but no longer flays raw with each breath. As seasons change and new memories form without their physical presence, what was once only sorrow will blend into a bittersweet nostalgia for all you treasured in them. They may no longer reside beside you tangibly, but their impact and role in shaping who you are can never be undone or taken away.

While goodbyes give closure, it's the eternal imprint your memories leave on your heart and soul that truly keep someone alive long after physical death has occurred. Concentrate on nurturing that unbreakable inner bond to find comfort within yourself whenever missing them grows unbearable. With patience and care for healing, what was once only pain will transform into a warm respite found through fond remembrance of loved ones immortalized by the imprint left on your heart.

Making It Real

Nothing can fully prepare you for the stark reality of losing someone you love. Even after being told about a death, your mind continues grasping at the only reality it's known up until then—one where that person was still living, part of your everyday life.

Malik was experiencing this firsthand after his beloved grandfather suddenly passed away in a freak accident. Every Friday, like clockwork, Grandpa picked Malik up from school to spend weekend adventures or afternoons together. That weekly ritual gave Malik something joyful to look forward to amid the stresses of classes.

But now, on the first Friday without him, Malik felt lost. Where was he supposed to go with no grandpa? The future he'd planned on was ripped away, leaving this cold, empty feeling instead. Coming home alone after school instead of going with Grandpa brought an unexpected wave of fresh sorrow.

Malik's room became his refuge from the hurt. But by lying in bed, dwelling on memories, he couldn't numb the pain entirely. He kept replaying Grandpa's last moments before the fall, filled with anger that some twist of fate stole them from making future plans come true. Why did it happen at all? It didn't seem right or fair.

When Grandma called to invite him over, Malik declined. How could he face being there without Grandpa? His normal way of coping with loss so far has been solitary grieving to avoid outwardly showing vulnerability. But Grandma cut through his assumptions, reminding Malik that even after loss, those left behind take comfort in each other.

Her wise words made Malik realize his absence now might bring more pain than trying to move forward together. Grandma understood the feeling of sadness; she missed her husband of 35 years tremendously too. But keeping traditions alive was how their connection survived, even without their physical presence.

Upon arriving, Grandma passed Malik their old photo album, filled with snapshots of family memories through the decades. Looking through pictures of happier times when Grandpa was still around brought mixed emotions. It hurt to miss that past laughter so sharply, yet it was comforting to see how big a role Malik played in bringing Grandpa joy over the years.

As evening fell, Malik shared his favorite Grandpa story with Grandma and his little brother—the time they fell into a giant leaf pile, laughing while jumping in together. Seeing their smiling faces, Malik realized reminiscing ensured those precious bond-building moments continued to echo even after the person was gone. Recalling fun times together kept Grandpa's spirit in their hearts whenever missing him grew too heavy.

With Grandma's encouragement, Malik began opening up more about his feelings of anger, regret, and confusion over Grandpa's sudden death. She reassured him that accidents are never planned or predicted so no one could have prevented what happened. The only thing within Malik's control now was the choice to keep honoring Grandpa's memory through fond remembrance.

As more visits passed, Malik started to accept the uncomfortable dichotomy—while physically gone, Grandpa remained very much alive through the impact he left in shaping their lives together. With time and care from loved ones helping him grieve, Grandpa's presence transitioned from something stark and missing to someone whose love and lessons continued brightening his days.

The first Friday without Grandpa will likely always carry some lingering sadness. But choosing to surround himself with others who cared for Grandpa showed Malik that even in death, circles of affection weave survivors together. As long as memories and traditions are preserved, those we've loved live on as much through the imprint they leave on us as any earthly interaction ever could. Though hard lessons to learn so young, Malik began finding solace and strength in moving forward.

What Am I Supposed to Do Now?

When death strikes, it shatters your whole worldview—suddenly, a future you imagined isn't possible anymore because that important person isn't in it. You're grieving the life you thought you'd have with them in it.

So, it's completely normal in those first days and weeks to feel utterly lost, as if you don't know which way is up anymore.

Your mind races with anxious questions like, *What do I do now?* and *How do I keep going without them?* There are no easy or quick answers; sadly, grieving is an incredibly long and difficult process with many ups and downs along the way.

The most important thing is to give yourself permission to fully experience whatever emotions come up and take all the time you need to mourn. Don't try to rush or suppress your natural grief. Cry when you're sad and yell when you're angry—let it all out in a healthy way. Suppressing feelings will only make healing harder in the long run.

It may seem strange, but find comfort in sharing memories of your person with others who knew them too. Remembering funny stories and favorite moments together keeps the good parts of them alive even when their physical presence is gone. Hold onto mementos that remind you of their life and the impact they had on yours—pictures, cards, notes, voicemails, anything to help recall the joy they brought you.

Talk about them still, even if just to yourself. Narrating memories out loud or writing them down ensures details stay anchored in your mind so you don't forget tiny, special things. Speak their name as if they can hear it; it lets your person know they're still deeply loved and not forgotten, which helps soften the pain of loss over time.

Focus on ways you can continue their legacy. Maybe that means volunteering for a cause they cared about, achieving a dream they supported you in, or being someone others can confide in the way you did with them. Finding purpose by honoring them is comforting.

Realize that no matter your intense pain now, life does go on, and eventually, the urge to live will outweigh the urge to die of a broken heart. Time makes sorrow more manageable, though the scar will remain. Be patient and gentle with yourself as healing happens at its own pace.

When you're having crisis-level thoughts about death or are unable to function, please tell someone you trust right away. Reach out to a counselor or doctor or call a grief support hotline any time of day or night. There are people who want to ensure your safety and help you bear this load until you feel steady enough again. There's courage in asking for help; it doesn't mean you're weak, just human.

Remember that while sudden or senseless loss may challenge your faith or worldview, you can find strength even in darkness' depths. Your loved one would want you to keep living life to the fullest in their memory however it works best for you. Day by day, choice by choice, you can rebuild a new normal where their unbreakable love remains to lift you through all of life's seasons yet to come.

Chapter 3:

Navigating Change—

Facing Challenges

All of us will experience change at some point in our lives. Whether it's the loss of a friend or even a loved one, every change takes something away from us. This leaves us feeling empty, confused, and unsure about what will happen next. Navigating change after experiencing a major loss can feel overwhelming. It's common to have a lot of questions swarming your mind, like *Who will I talk to now?* or *Will I have to move?*

Death is one of the toughest kinds of losses we can face. It can feel like part of you is now missing forever. Your mind may be flooded with memories of happy times you shared with that person or thoughts of all the things you'll never get to do or say to them again.

All the normal daily activities you took for granted before now feel strange and painful without them around. Simple things like eating meals, watching TV shows, or hanging out with friends are now reminders that your loved one is gone. It's really common to feel like a part of your routine, identity, and even yourself is gone too after losing someone. This sense of emptiness can be incredibly difficult to cope with.

These feelings are normal reactions to an abnormal situation. Grief is a natural and healthy response to significant loss. While grief isn't easy, it shows how much value and meaning that person brought to your life. Allowing yourself to feel the pain, sadness, and emptiness is the only way to truly heal over time. Trying to ignore or suppress those feelings will only make it harder to move forward healthily.

The changes that come from loss can challenge us in many ways, but it's what we do with those challenges that really matter. While change may at first seem scary and unwanted, it also offers opportunities if we allow it. One truth about change is that it's inevitable; we have no choice but to face it, accept it, and find ways to adapt. Sometimes this means making difficult adjustments, like moving homes or schools. Other times, it means finding new routines and ways to honor someone's memory.

Whether big or small, every change requires effort and strength from within. Leaning on loved ones for support during this tough transition period is important too. Allowing others to help lighten your burden instead of trying to navigate changes alone is a sign of courage not weakness. Their understanding words, comforting hugs, or even just their solidarity in shared memories can help you feel less isolated in your grief

Though the challenges of change may feel overwhelming at times, it's comforting to know you don't have to face them alone. Sharing your emotions with trusted friends or finding an empathetic grief counselor are great options if you need extra help coping. Their guidance can help ease fears, provide different perspectives on change, and give insight on healthy grieving practices. With time and support, the initial feelings of emptiness from loss slowly morph into fullness from treasured memories.

Change is rarely easy, especially after significant losses that shake our world. But challenging times often lead to personal growth if we're open to learning from them. While a part of who we were before is now different, focusing on what remains—our determination, faith in ourselves, and loving bonds with others—helps build our foundation for whatever future changes lay ahead. Staying hopeful, asking others for help readily, and making changes one step at a time eventually lightens even the heaviest of burdens. With patience and perseverance, you will adapt and come to accept changes as a natural part of life once again.

The Loneliness of Grief: Feeling Disconnected From Your Peers

Grief has a way of isolating you, even when you're surrounded by people. After experiencing a major loss, everything in your world seems to change overnight. The person who always took care of things is suddenly gone, and you don't know who to call when you need something.

Simple daily tasks that used to be easy now feel confusing and overwhelming. Even being with friends can make you feel alone because it seems like no one fully understands what you're going through. All the normal daily activities and routines you used to enjoy now feel empty and are hard to care about. It's like a part of you has been left behind while the world keeps moving forward without missing a beat.

This sense of being disconnected and having life pass you by is one of the loneliest parts of grief. Though family and friends want to help, the void and worries in your heart aren't easily fixed. Their daily thoughts and concerns may not always match up with yours. People expect you to get back to normal quickly, but grief has no timeline.

While their support is appreciated, it's also isolating when others don't truly comprehend your inner suffering. Comments like "It's been a month already; you should be feeling better by now" don't ease this loneliness; they often make it feel worse. You might withdraw from spending time with peers as a result, which only deepens the feeling of being alone.

It's natural after a loss to lose interest in activities you used to enjoy and sometimes struggle to focus your thoughts. These too are normal parts of grieving, yet peers may misinterpret it as you not caring about friendships anymore. Their lack of patience in trying to rush your grief journey can breed more loneliness.

While friends mean well, it's important to communicate your feelings honestly without fear of hurting others or being seen as bringing down their moods. Sharing how much a simple outing or school assignment now exhausts you emotionally goes a long way toward building understanding. Wanting time to yourself doesn't necessarily reflect how much you value your friendships, but explaining yourself helps curb feelings of abandonment.

With understanding comes the realization that this painful period need not destroy bonds; it may instead strengthen them through mutual support. True friends make space for your grief and honor it, even if they cannot truly relate. Simply having friends be present, showing care and patience without words, is a comfort and helps ease the loneliness.

Though reaching out takes courage amid sorrow's depths, isolating yourself further delays healthy coping. This is the time to be upfront about your needs, set limits on days when heavy conversations won't help, and accept help graciously when the darkness closes in. Friends willing to listen without advice, sit quietly in shared silence, and check in regularly with genuine care become lifelines of comfort rather than reminders of your differences.

Keep the lines of communication open through honest feelings shared sparingly. Note positive interactions and small kindnesses, however imperfect, done for you during difficult days as they help remind you of your bonds' endurance through difficult seasons. Time and patience on all sides brings clarity, determining whether relationships will deepen or are not meant to last on this journey.

While navigating grief alone may seem safest at first, relying on trusted loved ones to walk beside you lightens loneliness's load. Their simple presence affirms that you are not forgotten or set apart while healing. Together, you help each other discover life's continuity amid loss's disruption, and your connections are strengthened through facing sorrow side by side. Though loneliness comes, it need not conquer or define you when you reach out from grief's isolation with compassion.

This is also a time to be gentle with yourself. Keep healthy habits like eating nutritious meals, resting adequately, limiting distracting screens, journaling freely, and exercising safely outdoors. Focusing on self-care amid grief's intensity prevents further spiraling and allows you to nurture whatever inner strengths surface through facing immense challenges. Spending quiet moments showing gratitude for even the small mercies witnessed each day repositions your perspective.

Moving Forward, Not Moving On:
Integrating Grief Into Your Life

While the past cannot be regained, the future remains unwritten. We have a choice in how we move forward, whether living bound by grief or in gratitude for lessons learned. Though it seems harsh, the world keeps turning despite our private sorrows. Life goes on, requiring us to resume responsibilities and adapt to changing family roles. This does not mean that moving on implies forgetting or dishonoring precious memories. Rather, it's finding a new normal integrated with their enduring influence on who we became because of them.

Don't feel guilty about taking steps toward healing, like engaging in interests or pursuing relationships again. Your loved one would want you to live fully despite their absence rather than be defined by loss. While the darkness will visit in grief's depths, opening your heart to moments of joy again honors the precious time you shared. Dark isolation delays healthy grieving's progression, but reclaiming a balanced life fuels renewed purpose.

With the perspective brought by time, we learn to hold special connections within our hearts rather than externalize them through possessions or places. Their memory becomes portable wherever we go. Small rituals like dedicating achievements, wearing favorite colors on anniversaries, or remembering milestones together privately keep a bridge between the past and present. Creative outlets such as writing letters, compiling photo books, or tending a garden in their honor provide solace.

Sharing fond memories and feelings about your loved one with family can really help keep their memory alive in a caring way.

As time passes, even if it's still hard sometimes, talking to other loved ones can bring everyone a lot of comfort. Hearing happy stories about what they were like, funny things they used to do, or little ways they showed their love and support let their spirit live on in all your hearts. What may have felt too difficult to talk about at first can actually turn into a soothing thing. It has a way of bringing everyone even closer during the saddest of times.

It's definitely not easy to figure out a new normal after losing someone who was such a big part of your family. Changing routines and finding your place with people grieving differently can be hard. But taking things slow with patience, keeping communication honest but caring between everybody, and being willing to bend the rules a bit here and there to make everyone less stressed also strengthens relationships in the long run. And starting new traditions or little things you do together that respectfully include remembering loved ones who passed while also celebrating each other now can really help too. As long as you pursue your own growth and goals with continued thoughtfulness for your people through tough times—like they probably taught you their whole lives—it honors what they gave up so you could be here and be your best self.

Carefully consider what aligns with your loved one's dreams for you before guilt or anger stunts life's unfolding. Their hopes were for your happiness not imprisonment in a gray past. Appreciate the assistance of counselors, support groups, or religious communities to gain perspective on transitioning identities while staying close to core principles absorbed from your loved one.

Though months and years lessen outward displays of mourning, the grief never disappears; you integrate it by accepting life's constant changes gracefully. Be patient and compassionate with yourself through setbacks, using challenges more as teachers than failures. Choose growth by reflecting on how your loved one faced hardships with courage, humor, and mercy for themselves and others.

Making It Real

Andrea couldn't believe it had been a month already since the night of the party when her best friend Melody was shot. Each day since felt unreal, like she was stuck in a nightmare that refused to end. Melody was the only person who truly understood Andrea. While other kids at school had lots of friends, Andrea always felt like an outsider until Melody befriended her in her freshman year.

Melody brought Andrea out of her shell. She helped Andrea feel confident about her creative talents when others made fun of her art projects. At Melody's urging, Andrea started an Instagram account showing off her jewelry designs. With Melody's encouragement and compliments, Andrea's tiny following grew to over a thousand within a year. For the first time, Andrea found positive validation in her skills and didn't feel weird among her peers.

Without Melody, Andrea felt alone and isolated again. A heaviness had settled in her chest that wouldn't lift no matter what she tried. Even getting out of bed each morning became a Herculean task as she faced the meaningless activities of each day without her biggest supporter by her side. Andrea began withdrawing from everyone, skipping classes to hide in the library at lunch where no one would look for her.

Andrea's sudden change in behavior did not go unnoticed by Mrs. Fernandez, the school guidance counselor. When she called Andrea to her office a few weeks after Melody's death, Andrea expected a lecture on truancy. Instead, Mrs. Fernandez gently acknowledged Andrea's grief and loss while expressing care for her well-being. She set up weekly check-ins for them to discuss how Andrea was coping and any strategies or resources that could help.

At first, Andrea didn't see how talking would solve anything. The heaviness and emptiness inside couldn't be talked away. But Mrs. Fernandez listened patiently, without judgment, as Andrea spilled her aching heart over the following weeks. She spoke about how Melody was the one true friend who accepted her completely for who she was. With Melody gone, Andrea felt untethered and alone, facing each day without her rock by her side.

Slowly, the counseling sessions began taking some of the weight off Andrea's shoulders. Mrs. Fernandez helped her see grieving as a process—not something to push away but something to face gradually with self-care and healthy coping. She located low-cost evening classes in jewelry making and encouraged Andrea to enroll. At first, Andrea resisted, not wanting to replace Melody or disrespect her memory by enjoying a hobby they both loved without her.

But Mrs. Fernandez gently affirmed that honoring someone's memory didn't mean isolating from life or things you both cherished. Taking comfort in an interest they shared kept Melody's spirit alive rather than dishonoring it. Gradually, the idea of channeling her sorrow into art began bringing Andrea comfort rather than guilt. She signed up for the six-week jewelry class and was surprised to find the instructor and fellow students were a supportive group who lifted her mood each session.

Creating colorful beaded bracelets gave Andrea's hands something to do during times when her mind replayed the tragedy on a loop. She poured her memories and grief into each design, coming to see them as gifts her creativity crafted with

Melody's inspiration behind them. The weekly classes gave her something positive to focus on and look forward to. Her growing pile of "Melody Inspiration" bracelets became treasures she shared proudly with Mrs. Fernandez and eventually her parents to show her progress.

By honoring their special friendship in a way that was meaningful to them both, the bracelets helped make Melody and her memory feel real again after the numbness of early grief. Over the next few months, with Mrs. Fernandez's guidance and the creative outlet of her jewelry, Andrea began slowly adding words and then actions to her ongoing journey of grieving. Her smiles started coming more easily on some days as fond recollections outweighed the sadness. She reached out to volunteer to help younger students in the art club, finding purpose in paying forward Melody's kindness to her.

Andrea knew deep sorrow would visit for life's milestones without Melody, but through choosing courage each day to keep living fully rather than shrink inside her pain, Melody's light continued to brighten her path ahead. While perfect happiness remained in the past, moments of contentment and even occasional laughter were attainable once more in the present by honoring her dearest friend's memory by living the dreams they once envisioned together. With ongoing support, Andrea's way of grieving healed and transformed her self-perception from a solitary outsider into one lifted up and empowered by another's goodness to walk stronger into an independent future.

What Am I Supposed to Do Now?

Losing someone you care deeply about turns your world upside down in an instant. One moment, your daily routines and future plans included that special person. The next, they are suddenly gone and you are left wondering, *Now what?*

It's a scary and confusing time full of changes you never expected to face alone. Important decisions can no longer be put off, but grief also makes it hard to think clearly. Take time before making any major life choices when deep sorrow clouds your mind. Discuss options with trusted family and listen to different viewpoints before committing to a big change like switching schools or careers in haste.

If one parent or both are gone, responsibilities around the house will need to be shared in new ways. Reassure your younger siblings that you will all support each other through the hard times ahead. Accept help from loved ones willing to cook meals, offer rides, or take on chores alongside you as you adjust to changing family roles. No one expects you to cope or adapt alone right away.

Dealing with finances, insurance, estate planning, or other legal issues related to passing can feel overwhelming in grief's depths. Don't struggle silently through paperwork and confusing documents. Seek guidance from a lawyer or financial advisor after explaining your loss. An expert can simplify complex matters and ensure important steps aren't missed during this vulnerable period.

Returning to studies or a part-time job soon after a loss requires care. Though routine and distraction hold appeal, avoid rushing back without advice. Speak to counselors or teachers about potentially taking time off if concentration lags or stress spikes. Going back gradually on a trial basis with flexibility allows for prioritizing self-care until stability returns.

Keeping a journal of fond memories, feelings, and milestones in grief's unfolding journey may bring comfort years later when sadness visits. Write freely without concern for style, remembering even simple days shared together or life lessons learned from your loved one. Compiling little things at risk of being forgotten over time helps sustain their legacy.

Consider joining an online or local grief support group for companionship with others on similar paths. Open up cautiously, but listen attentively to others' experiences in facing challenges like guilt, anger, or complicated anniversaries ahead. Diverse stories normalize varied reactions to sorrow while modeling hope found through enduring difficulties.

Make time to nurture happy recollections amid grief's shadows. View old photos of laughter shared or record favorite tales to preserve their character for future generations. Focus on positive qualities and joyful times rather than despair over what will never be again. Your loved one's goodness lives on in who you became because of their guidance and the love you received.

My friend, though the future ahead seems bleak now, with patience and community you will rediscover purpose again in time. Remember, grief teaches that darkness cannot drive out darkness; only light can do that. By slowly integrating your loss while prioritizing tender self-care each day, lightness will touch your path more and more as you honor their memory through living fully. You are stronger than you know and will overcome present struggles by supporting one another with compassion. Chin up; brighter days are coming.

Chapter 4:

Finding Your Own

Way to Grieve

You've now spent some time allowing yourself to feel whatever emotions have come up as you walk this painful path of grief. Remembering what I shared before about ups and downs being normal, I want to talk to you now about finding your own way through.

Grief affects everyone differently; there is no right or wrong way to feel sad, angry, or confused after losing someone important. In the same way, how you handle those difficult emotions that come is also not a one-size-fits-all thing. What helps one person may not help another, and that's perfectly okay. The most important thing is choosing support that works for you.

There are so many sources of support out there, so I want to help you think about what might be most helpful for where you're at right now. Counseling with a grief therapist is one option many teens choose. Speaking to someone who really understands grief can feel really good. It gives you a safe space to share all your feelings without holding anything back.

If the idea of one-on-one counseling seems scary, there are also peer support groups run by charities or hospitals just for teens going through similar losses. Being with others your age who truly get what you're experiencing is comforting in its own way.

You can support each other with hugs and understanding when words aren't enough.

If spirituality or faith helps you make sense of life and death, your church, temple, or community center likely offers grief workshops and seminars too. Having clergy members to lean on who believe in an afterlife can feel grounding and hopeful. Prayer, meditation, or rituals related to your religion may provide peace as well.

Spending time with close family and friends who really knew the person you lost can also aid healing. Whether cooking together, looking at photos, or just sharing funny stories, those bonding moments with others who cared about them remind us we are not alone in our grief. Their hugs communicate compassion when words fail.

Creative arts therapies may appeal to you if you find expression through music, dance, painting, or writing. Whether joining a grief camp focused on theater, music, or DIY projects or exploring independently at home, creating art allows emotions and memories to flow freely from our hands into meaningful pieces.

Nature can work wonders too. Going for long walks with your pet, hiking up hills, and breathing fresh air while soaking in natural beauty grounds and re-centers our thoughts. If being active helps you cope, community sports teams or dance classes welcoming all ages may appeal.

Remember, the options are wide and varied; it's okay if none of the above really speaks to your personality or needs right now. You get to choose what feels most right for where you're at in grieving your person. Try things out one at a time or mix and match types of support if that suits you best. And it's perfectly fine to switch things up as time passes if your wants and needs change.

One universal thing I'd suggest is keeping a journal just for your grief. Writing letters to your loved one, pouring out feelings, or writing about memories is very healing. It gets emotions out of your system without burdening others. And you can return to entries whenever you want or need reassurance that your emotions are normal and valid.

Finding your people and support methods will be an ongoing process of listening within. But those small steps make such a difference. They remind us we don't have to journey alone and there are caring listeners ready if we want help to carry us through sad or angry days. The heart knows healing happens gradually through leaning on others' compassion. And that caring help is there for you whenever you decide you need it.

Remember, there is no timeline here. Go slowly, try things, and see what works for where you are today—that's all that matters. Promise yourself patience and grace as your heart finds its way, one understanding step after another. Your healing is a beautiful, lifelong journey that you get to craft uniquely for yourself.

Your Grief, Your Rules: Exploring Different Ways to Grieve

No one grieves the exact same way. We all deal with loss in our own unique way. What's important is allowing yourself to feel what you feel without judging yourself or comparing how you grieve to others. As long as you're not putting yourself in danger, there are no right or wrong ways to grieve.

When someone important passes away, it can seem like the sadness will swallow you whole. And that's understandable—it hurts so much to lose someone you love. But while grief may always be a part of you, it doesn't have to control your whole life. Grieving is about adjusting to life without that person not getting stuck in never-ending sadness. It's a process that takes time, but you can learn healthy ways to let your feelings out while also taking steps forward.

Different Grief Styles

People have different natural grief styles based on their personality and what feels comfortable. Some common styles are:

- **Emotional:** letting feelings out by crying or yelling. This helps release emotions rather than bottling them up.

- **Task-focused:** keeping busy with work, chores, or hobbies to distract from the pain. Getting things done can be a way to feel in control.

- **Social:** leaning on family and friends for comfort by sharing memories. Talking through feelings provides support.

- **Spiritual:** finding meaning through faith or personal beliefs. This could mean prayer, scripture, or reflection.

- **Independent:** needing alone time to process inward versus outward emotional expression. Writing feelings down privately can help.

No style is better than another; it's about understanding yourself and honoring how you naturally cope. Mixing methods is also common. The goal is to care for your mental health by confronting grief without ignoring it or getting stuck in sadness.

Various Ways to Grieve

Everyone's relationship with the person they lost is unique. So, how you grieve that person will look different too. There are many options to consider:

- Attend a grief support group with others going through similar losses. Sharing experiences can help reduce isolation.

- Make a memory book, scrapbook, or video filled with pictures, cards, and mementos from your time together. Laughing through old photos is therapeutic.

- Plant a tree or a garden or create another living memorial in remembrance. Nature provides calm and a symbol of new life even after death.

- Participate in fundraising for a cause related to their illness or donate to an organization they cared about. Helping others is empowering when you feel helpless.

- Visit places where you shared happy memories, like community spots, concerts, or vacations. Surrounding yourself with familiar things provides comfort.

- Light a candle, say a prayer, play their favorite song, or do something that feels respectful. Small rituals create space to honor them.

- Write letters to the person who passed, expressing all your thoughts and emotions, even if they won't receive them. Putting your feelings on paper can lift a weight off your heart.

- Make a dream board or vision collage of things you want to experience or accomplish in memory of their legacy and life lessons. Set goals to move forward.

While grief looks different from day to day, there are always options to process it by finding a balance between remembrance and healthy distraction. Try different coping methods to see what brings you comfort as you learn to carry on living well despite such a big loss.

Coping With Ups and Downs

Grief isn't a smooth, linear process; it comes in waves, as we discussed in earlier chapters. Expect good and bad days as you adjust to life without that special person. Some days you'll feel okay and others the sadness may floor you. That's normal. Be gentle with yourself through the ups and downs.

It typically takes around two years for acute grief to lessen after a significant loss, like a parent or sibling. But grieving isn't time-bound; it's more about going through emotional phases at your own pace.

Revisiting earlier phases isn't a failure; every milestone reached is progress. Anniversaries and holidays exacerbate grief too. Commit to your self-care through these times by surrounding yourself with loved ones, talking to a counselor, or leaning on your support system.

Though change is hard, each day you keep going is a testament to the impact they had on your life. Choosing to honor their memory by living well, as difficult as it seems, is how their legacy lives on through you.

Grieving can feel lonely, but you don't have to do it alone. Reach out any time you want to talk, think of memories together, or need a shoulder. Friends and adults who care understand that everyone grieves differently. Over time, though that deep hurt never fully leaves, their role in your heart transforms from heavy pain to the joy they brought you. Keep learning and growing, even through some of life's hardest chapters.

While the person is gone physically, choosing to remember their most cherished qualities helps that meaningful relationship continue spiritually. Most importantly, honor that special person by living your best life each day, which is the ultimate testament to how they impacted who you are. As long as you continue to grow through grief rather than stay stuck, you're doing it right on your terms—your grief, your rules.

Finding Solace in Rituals: Creating Meaningful Traditions

Grief can feel like a heavy storm cloud following you everywhere on gray, rainy days. When someone important to you dies, it's normal to feel totally lost, sad, and confused. Your mind and heart ache from missing that person. Getting through each day may seem impossible at times. I know how exhausting it can be to constantly feel all the ups and downs of grief.

While there's no magic fix to make the pain disappear, creating some rituals and traditions can help give your grief a routine path to walk. Having certain times or activities set apart just for honoring memories or letting out feelings may provide comfort when you need it most. Rituals can be simple things you do regularly to feel closer to the person you lost. They don't have to be perfect; the things that make them meaningful are that they're thoughtfully chosen by you.

Some people like lighting a candle at dusk each night to reflect on a loved one. Others may look at old photos or play their favorite song. Planting a special garden or volunteering for a cause they cared about are also gentle ways to keep connecting. Think about things you enjoyed doing with that person or small acts that remind you of who they were. Then set aside certain days or times weekly to do similar things alone or with others who knew them too. Rituals don't need to be grand; tiny, thoughtful moments can nourish your grieving heart the most.

One ritual many find comforting is writing letters. You don't have to send them, but putting your ongoing grief journey and memories into words on paper is healing. Others find solace in journaling each day's emotions or recording their favorite stories to listen to again when missing them hits hardest. Scrapbooking with mementos or keeping a dedicated box, shelf, or area solely for that person is another way to honor their life. Lighting a small candle just before bed or leaving a flower by their photo each morning can feel like a comforting hug during hard moments.

Getting outdoors when missing your loved one is a simple ritual that you might appreciate. Going for short walks, hikes, or bike rides to peaceful spots you enjoyed together naturally lifts thoughts heavenward. Bringing along a playlist of their favorite tunes or pausing at special places allows space to reconnect and feel less alone. Sitting quietly beneath their favorite tree, stargazing where they showed you constellations, or picnicking in a park can softly soothe aching memories. Even light exercise like throwing a ball, dancing, or yoga during set days of the week dedicated to that person may ease tension.

Expressing grief through creative outlets is another kind of ritual that soothes many. Writing poems or songs, drawing portraits, photographing nature, or simply journaling colorfully can release emotions productively. Some make memory boxes of collected items, arrange photos artistically, or even start new hobbies the person encouraged. Others find comfort in volunteer activities they cared about or community service in their honor. Do what feels right for you; honoring their spirit through your unique gifts naturally lifts both your heart and soul over time.

Setting aside special occasions like anniversaries, birthdays, or other meaningful dates for reminiscing rituals helps ongoing grief feel less lonely too. Prepare their favorite meals, play their favorite music, or watch movies you enjoyed as a family. Look through scrapbooks, home videos, or simply light candles silently in gratitude for the gift of knowing them, even if only for a while. Inviting others who share your loss to casually get together on significant days also nourishes healing. Don't hesitate to lean on understanding friends and caring relatives; togetherness makes heavy burdens lighter to carry.

As the seasons change, consider setting up seasonal rituals as well. Make autumn wreaths or press flowers from spring garden walks. Pick berries for jamming or roast marshmallows under bright stars like you once did. Whether alone or with loved ones, making new traditions out of old happy times together thoughtfully redirects sadness into sweet remembrance over time. Some plant special bulbs, trees, or bushes each year as symbolic living tributes that bloom anew with hope alongside grief's deepest shades. Gentle activities done quietly in honor of your person naturally turn tears into smiles within months or years.

Grief takes as long as it takes, so be kind and patient with yourself through this special yet difficult process. While some days may feel dark with deep sorrow, rituals brighten the shadows by keeping that person's light shining within your heart. With regular care and thought, simple traditions gradually become lanes, guiding you away from grief's heaviest thickets onto softer paths where memories bless more than ache. Establish both mind and body nurturing routines when fatigue sets in; their loving spirit remains cheering you on to better tomorrows even now.

Take all the time you need. Though sadness may visit often at first, brightness will blossom anew with each new season if nourished through meaningful rites. Let your unique ways of remembering with love be your medicine. And should clouds ever cover the sun too long, remember that other caring hearts also grieve and would gladly walk beside you should darkness seem too deep alone. With one foot in front of the other through this journey's valleys and meadows, you'll surely reach sun-drenched lands again, where memories bring only comfort, never pain.

Express Yourself: Coping Strategies

Dealing with grief can feel like a huge, heavy weight on your heart that makes each step harder to take. Waking up sad and staying sad all day with tears that just won't stop is exhausting. It's so normal to feel overwhelmed and like you don't know how to keep going. Your mind and emotions may be spiraling with should-haves and what-ifs that won't give you rest. But there are many gentle ways you can start expressing yourself that don't require fancy skills or a lot of money. Small acts of releasing what's in your heart through things meaningful to you can help lessen grief's heaviest loads, mile by mile.

A very helpful tool is to write about how you feel and your memories of that person. It doesn't need to be neat or edited; scribbling heartaches onto paper is its own soothing balm. Many find comfort in penning letters to their lost loved ones, even if they are unsent. Filling journals with thoughts, poems, lyrics, or doodles is another great way to get feelings flowing outward so they don't sit choking your insides. Art therapy like coloring, sketching, or photography also uses creativity to get grief moving. Some like painting their storm of emotions or turning sad songs into artwork as a healthy outlet.

However you express it, know that, however messy or not perfect, the very act of getting out what burdens you provides immense relief. Tears allow your heart to spread its wings, even if only for a few moments. Over time, as you practice honest expressions of sorrow or joy, heaviness lessens and you see brighter pathways ahead despite dark days. Be gentle with yourself as you start your journey. Rome wasn't built in a day, and neither is healing. But keep choosing tiny steps outside yourself through whatever means let you release and reconnect at a pace you can walk. Comfort arrives with conscious, caring steps, however faltering at times.

Speaking of which, social support makes grief's winding trails much easier to tread. Check in with parents or caregivers you trust as carrying immense burdens alone grows exhausting quickly. Share favorite memories or simply sit silently, being present should tears come without needing solutions or fixing anything. Caring ears reflect light back into darkness without thinking your pain should end fast. Allow others' caregiving without always having to appear strong—togetherness lifts the heaviest rocks from aching hearts.

Relying on good friends who simply listen without judging or advising is very soothing. Laughter shared over coffee or doing silly acts releases feel-good endorphins despite lingering shadows. Hugging, holding positive spaces, or spending time in nature together eases your lonely, aching soul. Should solitude grow too thick, connecting to peers who also walk sorrow's tightrope through groups or online spaces allows you to find comfort together through shared tears, smiles, or simple silence.

Beyond close circles, volunteer your time and gifts to help others manage grief through giving something positive back to life and the community. Working through feelings alongside locals needing assistance breaks loneliness and makes a better world, which fuels light and lifts darkness inside. Nature therapy—doing light gardening work or small repairs for those not able—also shifts the view to see that you're not alone on this sorrowful plane. Grateful smiles and thanks received provide care balms where none were thought to exist. Your gifts mean most just as they are—allow others' appreciation without always measuring your smile or how fast sadness should lift for acceptance.

Time with spiritual mentors who listen without fixing or judging lessens grief's deep waters. Though faith may bring more questions than answers right now, wise ears simply hold space without forced fixes and honor unique experiences. Rituals of prayer, scripture reading, music, or silence provide calm waters. Rest weary heads when the roughest seas stir underfoot. Find strength through whichever quiet practices speak most to your journey.

Taking care of your mind and body amid grief's heaviest storms is most important too. Exercise through sports, long walks, dancing, yoga, or hiking away from worries is better than any pill. Fresh air and sweat ease the stresses from tense shoulders and tight chests. Be easy on yourself despite aching joints; even little things done for your health benefit greatly.

Choose small habits for yourself too, like protective sleep, nourishing foods, drinking lots of water, and limiting distractions, to cure loneliness. Focus on today not how far tomorrow is—each sunrise brings renewed strength. Your worth doesn't diminish if tears come more frequently than smiles some days. Be as gentle as a warm summer breeze to your grieving spirit; it's been through a lot. Keep choosing moments to care, express your emotions however it works best for you, and rely on other hearts also walking this winding valley. Brighter landscapes surely open ahead, though clouds may linger at times.

Making It Real

The rain fell softly outside Leah's bedroom window as she lay staring up at the ceiling, lost in memories. It had been one year ago today that the accident happened—one year since her whole world turned upside down in an instant.

She remembered it vividly—getting the frantic call from her mom while she was in class, not understanding her choked words through tears at first. Racing to the hospital in a blur, praying it wasn't true even as her heart knew. Then seeing his still, silent form through the doorway and crumpling to the floor as an anguished wail tore free.

All their plans and dreams shattered on the cold tile. She had thought they had forever—that James would be by her side through every milestone to come. They had talked endlessly about their future—college, moving in together, and marriage one day with kids and grandkids—a future that now could never be. A future that ended with blazing truck tires and a split-second decision going horribly wrong.

Now it was just Leah, alone, facing the future that seemed bleak without her person. The months after had passed in a fog as she went through the motions of life numbly, feeling like half of her was missing. She had shut down, avoiding relationships or plans for more than a week. Her friends and family worried but didn't know how to help—what could make such a wound ache less?

But Leah was tired of dwelling in an endless cycle of grief and wanted to start living again. She knew James would want that for her too. So, on the one-year anniversary of his death, she set out with a new resolve to let go of old pain and make something of the time she still had to honor his memory.

Her first step was visiting their favorite spot, a cozy little coffee shop a few blocks from school. Sitting in their usual corner booth with a warm drink, she let memories wash over her with a bittersweet smile. She could picture James across from her, making her laugh with some silly jokes as usual. Taking a deep breath, she opened her journal for the first time in months to finally write down all the things left unsaid.

Page after page was filled with tears and laughter, inside jokes, and future plans scribbled out. She told James everything she wished she had said that last day, thanking him for the time they had and apologizing for shutting down after. As the words poured out, a heaviness lifted from her heart, leaving room for new growth. This was the first step to healing—facing her grief and releasing it instead of bottling up the pain.

Over the next few months, Leah committed to small acts of self-care daily. She started running in the mornings before school, finding fresh air and exercising helped shift her mood. She joined the yearbook committee to stay busy and meet new people. Slowly, she started opening up to trusted friends about James and found comfort in their support. Going to a local grief group each week helped too, knowing others understood her pain in a way most couldn't.

On what would have been their anniversary, Leah and James' parents scattered his ashes at their favorite swimming hole as the sun rose. Trading tears and memories with James' parents brought her comfort, as did letting his spirit free in nature. That evening, the four of them had pizza and giggled at old home videos together, keeping his memory alive through love rather than sorrow. Leah realized that moving forward didn't mean forgetting the past; she was just carrying it in her heart instead of getting stuck there.

As senior year began and college acceptance letters arrived, another challenge arose. Leah had dreamed of attending their state school with James and getting an apartment nearby. Facing going alone shattered her heart anew. After much worry, she decided to go, knowing it was what James would want and that staying home wouldn't make the choice less empty.

Moving in felt bittersweet. Her new roommate Amy listened without judgment as Leah shared her journey, becoming a support. On campus, she slowly opened her heart to new experiences, people, and dreams beyond the past. As hard as it was not having James by her side, Leah found strength knowing a part of him still lived on in her memories and values.

The future was uncertain, but traveling grief's difficult road had taught Leah resilience she never imagined. She learned to live fully each day rather than fear plans changing; she found solace in everyday beauty rather than longing for what's gone. Her love for James still ran deep, just in a way less defined by his absence now. While a piece of her heart would always miss him, Leah realized she carried his belief in her wherever she went. He was with her in the lessons of life, not just locked in the past anymore.

Four years flew by as Leah focused on each moment. She graduated at the top of her class with a degree in elementary education, just like James had always known she would. As she faced new adventures in teaching and independence beyond college, Leah felt truly at peace with her journey. Her grief had transformed into gratitude for the love that guided her steps even now. And she knew without a doubt that James was proud of the strong woman she had become, able to live fully again while still honoring his memory in her heart each day. The clouds of sorrow had lifted at last.

What Am I Supposed to Do Now?

After losing someone deeply important to you, it feels like a huge part of your world has been turned upside down. The future you imagined is gone, replaced by so much uncertainty and pain that it's hard to see past the next hour, let alone figure out what you're supposed to do now. Everything seems different without that person by your side, and coping with their absence each day brings a whole new struggle.

The grief feels so heavy; it's like walking through knee-deep mud just trying to get through basic tasks. Your heart aches constantly and you flip between tears and numbness, longing for the wave of sadness to pass so you can breathe again. But the ocean of sorrow keeps crashing in relentlessly, drowning you anew every time you think you're finally surfacing for air.

It's completely normal in those early days and weeks to feel totally lost like nothing makes sense or will ever feel okay again. Your whole world has been shattered by this huge hurt, and putting the pieces back together seems impossible. Just getting out of bed each morning or making small decisions about the day feels like a monumental task when grief weighs so heavily.

But as time slowly passes, one thing you'll learn is that while grief never totally goes away, it does change shape. Those huge waves of despair that leave you gasping for breath will slowly start coming less often as you learn to cope. And you'll gain a new understanding that the deepest hurts in life also tend to grant us the greatest wisdom if we allow them to teach us.

The key is giving yourself full permission to feel however you need to feel in each present moment, without judgment or expectations about how long it should last. Some days you may find yourself crying for hours, while others have more stretches of calm. Both are completely normal reactions to loss, so don't put pressure on yourself to instantly get over it. Healing takes time, patience, and gentleness with yourself above all else.

Know that there is no right way to grieve either; each person's journey looks different. What works for one may not work for another, and different strategies may help on different days too. Figuring out which coping methods feel best for supporting your unique grieving process takes exploration. It's like buying clothes—you have to try different styles on to see what fits you perfectly in this new season of life.

Reach out to trusted loved ones for comfort. While you may want alone time, carrying such a huge hurt entirely by yourself will likely make it harder to bear long-term. Having others simply listen when you need to talk or offering caring hugs when tears flow provides light to dark places within. Don't shy away from relying on others; they want to help lighten what they can't remove for you.

Expressing your sorrow through various artistic outlets may also relieve weight from your heart over time. As we discussed earlier, channeling swirling emotions creatively redirects inward turmoil outward in a healing way. Journaling each day's tides of feelings or memories shared also calms stormy waters. There is freedom in honestly getting your internal thoughts out so they don't stay bottled up.

Physical activities you enjoy, like hiking, dancing, swimming, or team sports, are excellent ways to work through grief while caring for your well-being too. Fresh air, socialization, and exercise naturally lift heavy burdens, shouldering tired minds and bodies. Make sure rest and nourishment are also priorities as you travel this difficult road. Your grieving spirit needs extra loving care to endure each step forward.

As you determine which coping strategies fit your needs best, remember that what helps one day may not help the next. Allow room for trial and error; be gentle with yourself through changes and missteps. No path is perfectly straight after such a loss rocks your world. Have patience as you learn your new normal and the grace to pause on hard trails when needed until strength returns for the next leg of the journey.

Above all, don't put pressure on yourself to meet preset timelines for getting over it. Healing unpacks loss box by unique box, each requiring time and tenderness. Some days may seem like you take one step forward, two steps back— that's perfectly natural as your heart learns to carry on without its person. Allow all the feelings, keep choosing care for yourself through them, and have faith that brighter days will gradually become more frequent companions than not. You've got this, dear friend—one foot in front of the other, you'll walk through.

Chapter 5:

Taking Care of Yourself

Going through the grieving process can take a huge toll on you, both emotionally and physically. It's so important right now to make sure you're focusing on taking care of yourself. Your well-being needs to be a top priority as you cope with losing someone special. I know you must be feeling exhausted and overwhelmed at times. Grief is draining work!

When sadness or stress takes over, it can be all too easy to neglect your own needs. Things like eating right, sleeping enough, spending time with friends, and staying active might fall by the wayside. But those things are absolutely vital for getting through hard moments. Your mind and body need fuel to give you strength for emotional ups and downs. Remember that taking care of yourself shows how much you value your well-being. Make gentle compassion for yourself a daily goal.

One big part of self-care is setting boundaries. With family and friends offering support, it's important to create space for focusing on how you're feeling. Make sure others understand if you don't always feel up for company or conversations. It's okay to cancel plans when resting at home is what you need most. Be honest about your limits without apologies. Boundaries allow you to grieve freely without extra pressure.

Speaking of extra pressure, try your best not to take on too many responsibilities right now either. Grieving is exhausting enough without adding on homework, chores, events, or jobs. Your healing is too important; it's okay to sit out and say no to avoid feeling overwhelmed. Ask loved ones to help pick up the slack where you can.

Along those lines, don't be afraid to ignore messages or calls if chatting saps your energy. Returning messages can wait when closing your eyes for an hour means more. Let voicemails or texts pile up without guilt. You need to refuel however works best for you.

Something that can help is practicing mindfulness. When feelings wash over you, pause to focus on deep breaths to relax your body. Notice peaceful things like music or nature to gently distract your heavy heart. Meditation apps can help guide your calm moments too. These grounding techniques work to give anguished thoughts a rest.

The health of your friendships also matters throughout your grieving journey. Be wary of isolating yourself to avoid being a downer; spend time with caring folks who understand your feelings may fluctuate. Quality bonding releases stress hormones, even if grinning doesn't come easily yet. Socializing can be a form of self-care when you need it most.

Make extra effort with communication in your closest relationships, too. Your parents, siblings, or other trusted support system must know what you need from them each day. Don't be shy about sharing dark thoughts or good ones. Honest check-ins help them provide the healthy care you deserve without having to guess. Keeping others updated creates a strong support network.

Self-care also means honoring those you lost through positive means such as photos, music, or writing down treasured memories they gave you. Looking at photos of fun times together or listening to songs that remind you of them can bring a smile, even through tears some days. It keeps their memory close in a heartwarming fashion.

Most importantly, when it comes to caring for yourself, don't forget to be gentle with your healing heart. Grief will come in waves, so expect some rough shorelines ahead. Forgive yourself for your difficult feelings. Know that each storm will pass with patience and self-kindness as your captain. Honor your pace toward calm waters through nourishing moments at each sunrise.

Your well-being is so important. Taking good care of yourself looks different each moment; pay close attention to what your mind and body need at any given time. Balance food, rest, and social hours on a schedule you can commit to. You deserve to feel steady strength for your journey ahead. With compassion for where you're at each sunrise, you'll rise bravely through loss's toughest lessons. Stay strong yet soft in heart; this too shall pass.

Mind, Body, and Soul: Practicing Self-Care

Self-care means taking care of your whole self—mind, body, and soul. When you're grieving, it's so important to pay attention to how you're doing in all these areas. You need to tend to your emotional, physical, and spiritual well-being. Grief affects us deeply on all levels, so we've got to find positive ways to feed each part of who we are. That's especially true when heavy feelings weigh you down.

Learning what helps you process grief will make this journey a bit more gentle. One huge thing for self-care is allowing yourself to feel what you feel without judgment. It's so important to really acknowledge the emotions swirling inside during grief. Whether it's sadness, anger, fear, guilt, or anything else, let it move through you naturally without scolding yourself for feeling too much. Tell yourself every day, *It's okay to not be okay*. Saying those feelings out loud to yourself or in a journal can lift a weight off your chest.

Along those lines, really pay attention to what triggers bursts of feeling for you. What images, sounds, smells, activities, or anniversaries seem to make you overwhelmingly tearful or distressed? For some, it's grandma's recipes, dad's favorite music, or mom's perfume lingering in her closet. Knowing what sets off intense grief lets you gently prepare and tend to yourself with extra loving care on those days.

On that note, expressive writing can be so relieving and therapeutic. Grab a notebook or journal just for processing your grief experience. Write out memories, update how you're really doing instead of masking with friends and family, pen poems or letters to your loved one, and describe how you made sense of big emotions each day. Pour your heart out on paper as a release.

Meditation and mindfulness are very helpful practices, too. Take a moment to really check in with your breath and muscle tension using free apps that guide relaxation. Notice your body and mind in the present without harsh judgment and let your worries dissipate. Coming back to the here-and-now helps ease tightness in the chest. Short bursts are often effective if you struggle to focus for long periods.

Some extra soothing self-care is creating a playlist of songs that mirror your feelings. Tear up openly in your room with music that matches your sadness or reminds you of your loved one. Dancing freely can loosen pent-up feelings too. If music isn't your thing, making art, like drawings, paintings, or sculptures, can be very helpful in relieving grief. Getting those powerful emotions out eases them.

It's also great for your grieving mind and soul to connect with others who truly get where you're at. Look into peer support groups in your area for teens coping with loss. Sharing stories with folks the same age who also get what this is like creates an instant safe space to be real about your struggles without fear of being misunderstood. You can learn from others navigating similar waves.

Taking good care of your grieving body is key! Eat nutritious meals, even if you have no appetite. Get fresh air each day by going for walks outside. Do simple at-home exercises, yoga, or dance videos when energy levels vary. Stretching and strengthening the body and mind is self-care. Also listen to your body if it says rest is needed; curl up with a warm tea and ride out the low moments.

Above all, follow your intuition to calm your hurting heart. Pay attention to what truly soothes and uplifts you in each moment. You know yourself best; trust what feels right for a busy brain and heavy heart. Repeat calming practices to relieve tightness when sadness wells, hit replay on cathartic songs, sleep in some, or snuggle with fuzzy blankets. You're worth every bit of gentle care.

With practice and patience, all these self-care strategies can become your comforting toolbox for the hard days ahead. Learn about yourself and what lifts or settles your grieving moods. Honoring what your mind, body, and soul need through nourishing acts shows such bravery during tumultuous times. You've got this whole you—stay strong yet soft in heart; you're capable of rising up through the waves with room to feel it all fully yet find harbor each sunset.

Getting Help When You Need It: Reaching Out

Going through grief can feel so lonely and overwhelming at times. Even when surrounded by loved ones, the heavy emotions and struggles inside your mind and heart may leave you worn down. While self-care is important, you don't have to cope with or process your loss purely on your own. It's totally okay, and even wise, to reach out for extra support when sadness sinks its teeth in deep. Having people to lean on makes the ups and downs a little easier to ride out.

One thing to remember is that grief is a part of life. We all experience loss at some point, whether that's a family member, friend, relationship, or other type of loss. It's an absolutely normal human experience, as painful as it may feel. Knowing that grief is shared helps ease the belief that you're crazy or overreacting. When you're ready, speaking with others who understand your journey can provide tremendous comfort.

That's why seeking support from friends, family members, teachers, counselors, support groups, or other caring people is really important right now. While you don't have to burden one person with everything weighing on your mind and heart, having trusted people there in your corner lifts the load off your shoulders. Don't isolate yourself from the village that cares for you during your time of need.

Talking with close friends who bothered to learn about your loved one can help keep beautiful memories alive. Sharing happy stories or inside jokes through tears brings you closer too. Their big hugs have healing powers, even if they can't take your distress away. Remember, you can be a strength to others going through similar waves of hurt someday too.

Opening up to folks at school, like favorite teachers, is wise if heavy sadness or worries pop up between classes. Guidance counselors especially want you to find them any time sad, scary, or painful thoughts flood your brain too much. Their job is to support all students through life's challenges, big and small. No concern is minor in their eyes, so use them as a listening ear as needed.

Always feel free to check in with parents, siblings, grandparents, or other family members you trust, even if you simply say, "I'm really down today" to receive understanding before distracting yourself with activities together. Having someone aware of when low moments may surface means they're prepared to quietly sit with your tears or provide a distraction. Leaning on loved ones lifts the pressure to grin through the off moments alone.

When distress intensifies, truly consider speaking with a professional counselor or therapist. Guidance counselors can often connect you with low-cost local options available too. Support isn't only for the severely ill; grieving hearts going through massive change and emotional processing deserve empathy, coping strategies, and relief anytime sad clouds cover the sun. Therapy is a super safe space to unpack whatever weighs heaviest on you.

For added understanding, sign up for grief support groups in your school or area. Sharing stories and struggles with other teens navigating similar waters of sorrow can feel so soothing. Knowing you aren't alone in a confusing mix of feelings, not remembering details well, or having okay days followed by crying episodes normalizes what's really happening. Groups create an instant sense of belonging, with no awkward explanation needed about your journey. You uplift each other.

There are also online peer support communities if in-person meetings aren't quite comfortable yet. Many private Facebook groups or subreddits exist strictly for grieving individuals to bond over shared lessons and questions and celebrate milestones. Posting worries or seeking advice when sadness spikes lets supportive others offer gentle words through the phone, chat, or comments. The digital world has its place for connecting safely.

One thing I really want to say is that reaching out for help should never feel shameful. You wouldn't tell a friend with a broken leg to just cope alone, so don't put pressure on yourself to handle immense grief alone either. Accepting assistance makes you strong; it shows so much bravery and self-awareness to know when an outside perspective would benefit you. No one heals or copes perfectly. Treat yourself with the same understanding and care you would give someone going through a loss. You are deserving of help anytime, and however it appears, it uplifts you to climb from valleys. Remember, you define your own worth; it's not dependent on how much help you need.

Remembering to Live: Finding Joy Amid the Sadness

As the waves of grief come and go, it's easy to feel like your entire world has been washed away by the tide of loss. When someone you love is suddenly gone, it can seem unbearable to continue living without their presence. But the truth is that while your loved one may be physically absent, their memory and impact on your life remain. They would want you to keep experiencing all that life has to offer and not withdraw from living in their honor.

Remember that your loved one wouldn't want you to stop living fully because of their death. Even though they're gone, the ways they showed you to laugh, love, create, and appreciate each day still matter. Try focusing on how they brought light to your world and look for little reminders of their spirit in simple pleasures or acts of kindness from others. Carry their way of finding joy with you wherever you go.

While the grief may never fully go away, over time it will start to feel more like bittersweet memories you can smile about. Be patient yet persistent in seeking out what continues to nourish your soul each day, whether that's hobbies, time with certain friends, creativity, music, jokes, achievements, or adrenaline from favorite sports. Every little happiness feeds your courage to rise up a little more after tough times.

Sometimes, activities or hobbies that you shared with your person can feel comforting to do as a way of feeling close to them. Looking at old photos, cooking their favorite foods, listening to special songs, and working on projects you began are gentle ways to bond through joy again. And no one would fault you for occasional tears, but drying your eyes to laugh at funny shared memories feeds your light.

Another way to find small sparks of joy is to do acts of kindness for others in their memory. Whether volunteering your time, donating to causes they cared about, or encouraging friends struggling themselves, paying their compassion forward lifts you both up. Their spirit spreads more beauty in the world each time joy replaces someone else's tears too.

That said, be cautious of unhealthy coping mechanisms that promise escape from pain for moments only. While drinking, drugs, or reckless acts may temporarily numb raw emotions, they breed dangerous addiction or self-harm that actually increases distress in the long run. Hurting yourself won't bring your person back or ease the new void; it only risks leaving more loss behind. As hard as it is, you have to feel your feelings to heal without scars.

Instead, focus on activities that comfort and empower your whole self—things like exercising to tire out agitation, expressing creativity through art or music, investing in rewarding relationships, and practicing relaxing rituals like journaling, reading, baths, or nature walks. Taking good care of yourself replenishes instead of depletes. You're worth finding what feeds your soul gently each sunrise.

Perhaps the true way to find moments of joy is to understand how much your person would want your life to continue overflowing with love, smiles, and meaning, no matter when or how they pass. They gave you strength to rise through the roughest waves; now fly high with hope of better days ahead. While sadness will visit, happiness will embrace you again in time. Their memory fuels your light to shine on for others going through their own dark nights who might see you and feel courage rise up in their chest too.

Making It Real

April's story shows how deeply grief can affect every part of your life. From the moment her mom was diagnosed with cancer at just 10 years old, her entire world changed. For the next six years, she took on so much responsibility, caring for her mom while also trying to stay on track in school. In those formative years, her focus had to be on her mom's health instead of making friends and enjoying a carefree childhood.

When April's mom passed away, it left an enormous void. She had gotten so used to defining herself through her caregiver role that she had lost part of her own identity. With no friends to confide in about her experience, April struggled under the heavy burden of loss alone. Moving in with her grandmother, whom she barely knew, only amplified her feelings of isolation and being lost.

April's story shows how grief often creeps into every part of your life if you don't find healthy ways to process it. For her, certain days of the week held more painful reminders of loss due to her traditions with her mom. Saturday nights were torture as she dreaded Sundays without their weekly brunch ritual. The grief was always there under the surface, casting a shadow over little things many others likely took for granted.

This is where April's grandmother played a crucial role in her healing. Rather than letting April withdraw into sorrow, she encouraged her to reconnect with living through activities she enjoyed. By exploring hobbies like baking, April discovered an outlet for her creativity that also spread joy to others. Selling her cookies at school gave her a sense of purpose and a way to start rebuilding connections.

On those early Sundays, cooking still brought tears as well as smiles. But over time, the happiness of sharing her baked goods outweighed the sadness of missing her mom. Finding fulfillment through meaningful work is so important when grieving. It lifts you up at the same time as honoring your loved one by spreading their values of compassion.

April's story shows the importance of acknowledging exactly how and when grief hijacks us each day. By facing Saturday night fears head-on with support, she could mentally prepare for the pain of Sundays without her mom. Having a safe community at the grief group gave her space to admit struggles without shame too. With empathy and encouragement, you can learn healthy habits for navigating life's rollercoasters.

It's also inspiring how April learned to actively focus on happy memories and not dwell in the void left behind. Making the choice to remember joyful moments with her mom, like their brunch ritual, lifted the fog to see that light still exists after darkness. Her resilience to gradually rebuild her identity through hobbies, purpose, and connections despite the agony of early loss is so admirable. Her grandmother played a vital role in reminding April that, while her mom couldn't be replaced, happiness wasn't banished forever either. Joy can be chosen again through patience and a willingness to keep living fully in the spirit of the loved ones watching over us.

April's story shows grieving is not linear; it creeps into seemingly small spaces and resurfaces when least expected if not addressed healthily. But with self-care tailored to individual needs as well as an encouraging community, one can gradually rise to fly again after the hardest storms batter wings to the ground. April discovered an untapped inner strength to spread smiles rather than stay shackled by sorrows no one deserves to bear in solitude. Her story offers hope that any grieving soul can learn to bloom where once only darkness grew, with enough care and support, and a willingness to keep the heart open to the beauty of each gift that remains despite any curse of destiny that steals mother's wings too soon.

What Am I Supposed to Do Now?

When grief comes barreling into your life out of nowhere, it can leave you feeling utterly lost and alone. One minute your world was steady, the next it's turned completely upside down with no roadmap for how to cope or function again. With your person suddenly absent and all routines broken, anxiety swirls as you wonder, *What now?* It's normal to feel overwhelmed by the many unknowns ahead.

Please try not to be too hard on yourself during this disorienting time. Rebuilding after a tragic change requires immense patience and compassion, both for others as well as within yourself. While answers don't come easily, focusing inward to honor your needs will guide you gently through confusion. Lean into trusting your resilience to adapt and bloom where sadness tried creating a wasteland instead.

Simple small acts of care to nourish yourself will provide an anchor to weather emotional storms with grace. Have faith that however long it takes, light always finds cracks in even the darkest nights for those with eyes to see beauty there.

One step is tracking special days like anniversaries or everyday traditions you shared together. Circle birthdays, winter's first snow, movie night Sundays—anything that sparks memories. By marking these events on the calendar, you can avoid being blindsided by painful memories and give yourself space to feel these heavy emotions. Preparing helps you seize control over the natural grieving process over time.

Knowing your personal grief triggers empowers your self-care too. What images, scents, or locations reignite the deepest sadness? For some, it's favorite songs; for others, it's crowded halls or nature spots you explored together. Recognizing early signals lets you gently remove yourself from sources temporarily or brace your heart accordingly. Self-awareness breeds self-acceptance.

It's crucial to acknowledge and validate whatever emotions arise without judging yourself for tearing up while smiling or wanting to withdraw from chatting with friends. Grief affects us all differently, so trust that changing feelings are healthy and healing in their own perfect way. Say to yourself, *It's okay to feel sad, angry, numb, or all of it.*

Once the inventory of needs is clear, finding a safe space makes coping easier, like a cozy home base. This could be your bed, forest path, or studio, where releasing your true feelings won't shatter you further. Spend time absorbing surroundings that cater specifically to your identity and rebuilding in solitude.

Practice compassion always, especially for yourself during this transition that may bring regret, frustration, and fatigue. Speak to your grieving self with the same tenderness as your dearest friend in agony, gently accepting that internal critics will judge you harshest when being gentle is what's needed most. Your well-being deserves this precious care above all else.

Educating yourself about normal grief responses lets you normalize struggles and know you're not alone, weak, or enduring eternally. Attend community gatherings, read stories of others' transformations, or seek counseling to enrich your resilience toolkit. Knowledge is medicine when mixed with self-care tailored exactly to your needs.

Letting light penetrate darkness one sliver at a time, not all at once, may be the healthiest way through. Simple moments connecting to life sustained offer sanctuary—birdsong, crafting, sunrise running, soup shared beside loved ones who understand the heaviness in your chuckles. Let tiny bursts of brightness carry hope that the sun always rises again, even after the darkest nights. You've got this journey.

Chapter 6:

Creating a New Normal—

Looking to the Future

My dear friend, you have come so far in your journey of grief. I know some days the sadness and longing still feel as heavy as when you first received that devastating news. Your heart has endured more pain than any heart should have to. Yet you are still here, taking one step at a time, choosing to keep living in honor of their memory. That in itself shows what incredible strength of spirit you have.

While the deep grief may never fully leave, this is a chapter where we can start looking ahead again with hope stirring in our hearts once more. The future will never be the same as before they left us, but that doesn't mean it can't hold beautiful new beginnings too. It's okay to let yourself imagine what a new normal could look like for you now, even if all the pieces aren't clear yet. Your loved one would want you to keep pursuing your dreams and finding joy again.

Pursuing your hopes and talents is a wonderful way to keep their legacy alive through the impacts you make. The dreams they believed in for you still matter, and following them gives their love purpose beyond the grave. Continuing on the path you started together helps you feel connected. Even if the path ahead seems unfamiliar without their guidance, I know their spirit will walk beside you every step of the way.

Their memory deserves to be kept alive through your light continuing to shine for others. While it may feel scary to step into the future, doing so honors the precious gift of each new day they cannot experience with us anymore. We breathe deeper because they can no longer breathe at all, and we live fully for the moments they were taken from too soon. It's the ultimate way to transform even death's most painful sting into life's most beautiful tribute.

Don't feel shame if you have to start small, like picking up an old hobby again or reconnecting with joy's simplest sources. Going through the day without breaking down is an achievement to be proud of right now. You don't need to have all the answers or understand every feeling just yet. Keeping your heart and mind active assists in healing by giving your inner strength a chance to rebuild gradually over time.

Please don't lose hope; happy times can still lie ahead even if smiles don't come as easily yet. I know deep in your soul that they would want you to keep striving and fighting for your dreams, however rocky the road may seem. Rising each day is brave when darkness wants to pull us under. But you have a warrior's heart, and warriors never truly stop overcoming.

As you make small steps toward a new routine, know that it's perfectly normal if old hurt tags along or bad days still arrive without warning. Grief isn't a competition with time or something you can force. Allow yourself compassion through whatever tides you experience; you are stronger than you may feel. Your loved one believed in an entire future for you, and honoring their memory means keeping faith in that vision too.

Maybe for now, that simply means getting out into nature to heal your spirit, joining online support groups to know you're not alone in your sorrow, or finding comfort in old movies that make you laugh like you laughed together. Every little thing that nourishes your heart keeps hope ignited. And in time, as hope strengthens its wings inside you, you'll find renewed readiness to spread them further again.

Please remember that feeling love—it still being alive within you—is the most powerful way to overcome loss. Their energy gets carried forward through sharing that gift with the world, whether mentoring others coping with sadness too or supporting causes that brought you both joy. Let your greatest memories guide you in whatever direction they lead you. There, their hand remains holding yours.

This chapter, my friend, is about rising up to embrace another day and allowing their place in your heart to transform from a heavy stone to a bright guiding light again. I know if they could whisper to you now, it would be to tell you to open your arms to the future they bought you with their eternal love. The rest will follow in due course, as it should. But you will get there. I have faith in that courageous beating under your chest that just keeps going.

Choose to stand up straight and grasp life's next honest opportunity. After all, you have conquered many obstacles to still be here; nothing and no one can defeat the spirit within that dares to hope and try again. Your wounds will heal into scars that strengthen instead of weaken. Smiles will return in time, with all the memories still golden. But for now, if you keep your eyes on tomorrow, progress will follow. You've got this, one step at a time through every challenge. The dawn is yours, my friend, and so are all the dreams yet to come.

Let their legacy shine ever brighter as you shine, too. And may peace nourish your heart like summer rain nourishes parched earth once more. You are not alone. Now go, keep going, and let this next chapter begin.

Dreaming Again: Rediscovering Your Hopes and Dreams

As you continue journeying through this new landscape of life without your loved one's physical presence, it's so understandable that your dreams may feel further away right now than ever before. When their smiles lit up each day, hope came more easily too, but I know deep down, those hopes still beat within your heart, waiting to spread their wings once more.

It won't be simple, and some days their memory may make even wanting something feel like a betrayal. That's okay too; grieving is messy and nonlinear. But I'm here to tell you that rediscovering what inspires your spirit is so important for healing. Our loved ones wouldn't want us confined forever by sadness in a corner of our minds. They dreamed of seeing us soar.

Maybe right now all you see are the painful absences their passing left behind, or you find joy too bittersweet. But dreaming is the first step to realizing what really moves us without them physically here. And those dreams hold pieces of them we can keep close in a new way. They're a way of preserving some of what we had together instead of just memories that continue to fade with time.

It's alright if you need to take tiny steps at first, like picturing small hopes instead of big ones that feel scarier without their arms to run to. Start with something simple that calls to your soul, even if it's just reconnecting with an inspiring show or getting outside more each week. Nurturing small dreams can still transform us and bring light when nights feel lonely and long.

One idea that could help is writing down some of the plans and hopes you shared, even if they won't happen now as imagined. Looking through old messages about your dreams may spark new ideas. We can build new dreams on the foundations of what we wanted before sorrow came. Their essence stays alive in us to inspire the potential still ahead.

Maybe there was a trip you talked about taking one day or a skill you motivated each other to learn. Those dreams don't need to fully fade; why not find modified ways to experience these things in their memory? Whether a road trip exploring locations that felt meaningful or photography courses to capture new perspectives, the creativity of grief can birth dreams that soothe us as surely as they stir us.

You could honor meaningful places or events in changed yet still meaningful forms. What if their birthday became an annual day dedicated to planting a tree in their name, volunteering at a cause that touched their soul, or starting a new tradition to feel their spirit? Celebrating life in active ways is beautifully healing.

There's also power in sharing your journey to help others cope too. Whether starting a blog about grief and growth, joining bereavement groups to mentor others, or volunteering with crisis hotlines, your story could ignite a new purpose and help rediscover direction. Helping others heal what's already healed in you lifts the fog to see the light still there.

Most of all, try not to rush yourself or feel shame if tears come with dreams too. That shows how deeply you loved, and love still guides us onward. Give your heart time and patience, like a gardener tending to new growth. We can nurture hope in weeping and smile through the saddest days in their sacred memory.

Keep a journal of dreams old and new to look back on and see bright banners of possibility waving you toward tomorrow.

Share some memories and hopes that you've had, noting the progression over time of what brings rays of sunlight again into even the densest forest within. Our growth isn't linear; just keep walking and have faith that the dimmest trails lead somewhere wondrous too, in their own way.

Better days peek ahead, and you'll feel their light again when you're ready. For now, be gentle and let your grieving bring you guidance. Your soul knows the way, so trust what your broken yet resilient heart whispers it needs. Live lovingly and laugh when you can because our loved ones gave us the greatest gift by letting us keep on healing, learning, and finding our way in this beautiful world they can't see with us anymore.

Making Plans Without Them: Moving Forward With Confidence

As you continue walking this journey, I know how hard it can feel to imagine important moments that soon approach without them sharing in your triumphs. Our hearts naturally ache at the thought of new beginnings; their love cannot be witnessed in person as it once did. But I'm here to tell you that moving forward doesn't have to mean leaving them behind or dishonoring their memory; in fact, it can be a beautiful way to keep their spirit involved in your life.

Each milestone you reach from now on deserves celebrating, even if celebrating looks different without their hugs to run to. I promise that as scary as the future may seem without their physical support, you have so much wonderful potential to share with the world. Our loved ones loved us enough to want to see us spread our light regardless of distance or obstacles in the way now.

Their energy lives on through who you become and all the lives you'll touch tomorrow. So, please don't ever feel you need to lock your dreams away because one key part is missing now. Find ways to quietly include them instead so they remain a blessing walking beside you down new roads. The connections we make are eternal; what changes are temporary tears, not your heart's ties to all it has known.

Focus on carrying meaningful parts of them into anything you envision. What was their favorite meal or little things that made you both laugh together? Incorporate symbolic touches like that, which feel just right for different occasions. You could play their favorite song at an event or scatter a few of their favorite flower petals when taking photos—small moments to feel close without letting grief dim all the light.

When big upcoming days arrive, perhaps dedicate a special seat or space in your heart of hearts to know their spirit shares your joy, even if from a distance. Light a candle before something begins, and in your soul, hear them whispering how proud they are. Even on the toughest days, their love cannot be shaken, so let it keep uplifting you through everything.

Be brave by also giving yourself space to feel any emotions fully as they come at different points. Every milestone may reveal surprise waves of both happy and painful memories. Allow yourself to feel whatever rises without criticizing yourself; grief impacts us all uniquely, and there is no right or wrong way to respond as long as you aren't harming yourself.

Most of all, don't lose sight of the power your perseverance gives to inspire others through both triumphs and struggles ahead. By believing in tomorrow despite your sadness, you continue honoring their legacy while nurturing your own strength. While some tears may come, their love will remain your constant foundation to build upon for a fulfilling future.

You will get through this as you have already survived so much just to be here breathing today. Have faith that each sunrise unveils a new purpose and reasons to keep living fully, even though sorrow arrives too. Enjoy both laughter and tears because emotions make us the most real and alive. All feelings help us grow in beautiful ways we cannot foresee when clouds feel the darkest overhead.

My hope is that in time, through love, bravery, and compassion for yourself, gentle joyful moments will outweigh heaviness in your days' balance once more. Your light is needed and much in this world is still waiting to receive it. Our loved ones may watch from starry skies now, but their light remains as much a part of you as your own beating heart, keeping courage from fading.

Let that sustain you on any route ahead, whether graduating high school and starting a new chapter of life fresh or witnessing the milestones of children who will know their grandparents' memory and love through our words. Their memory can walk alongside us, bringing smiles to new generations too.

Each step you take honors all they brought to your life and reinforces that their belief in you was not mistaken. I know if they could, they'd be telling you now to lift your head high in pride, let each accomplishment bring gladness, and know you are never walking alone. Spread your wings bravely; your light is still too vibrant a gift to dim, my friend, and your tomorrow waits to embrace all your resilient heart can become.

Keep journeying in courage, but also remember that rest and compassion, as needed, are strength too. Have faith that new horizons will continue to unfold even on sorrow's roughest days, and let the warmth of living well nourish you through any coldness left behind now that they've gone home to Heaven's light.

Embracing Life After Loss: Finding Meaning and Purpose

As your heart continues to navigate this journey of deepest loss, I know the process of rediscovering meaning can seem hazy at times through grief's mists. It's only natural that this immense change may alter what once ignited your passions or outlook on life's purpose before sorrow entered your world. But I'm here to encourage you that even when our old dreams fade, new purpose wafts in on hope's gentle breath.

Within your story of strength and survival lies inspiration meant to uplift others through what you've overcome. Our loved ones live on in how we let their memory guide us to spread light wherever we walk this earth. While some paths look quite altered from before, know that your purpose remains as radiant as ever—it simply may reveal itself through shifted lenses of experience now.

Don't put pressure on finding all the answers immediately. For now, embrace each tender moment that brings a smile without analyzing why just yet. Let your soul wander wherever it uplifts without judgment. As feelings ease from wounds still unmended, quiet insights will come when you least expect them during life's simplest beauties, like embracing loved ones, enjoying art, or being outside in the sun's warm embrace.

Take your time rediscovering interests that stir creativity and meaningful connections. Perhaps music soothes your spirit or writing pours out feelings too big for words alone. You could explore volunteering at animal shelters, shadow others impacted by loss through youth boards, or capture nature's magic in poetry and photos to uplift online communities.

Even something as simple as picking up old hobbies again or venturing to parts of nature you both enjoyed can guide purpose's seedlings toward sunlight. Our loved ones stay alive in our shared love for life's small wonders that nourish us. In honoring them by living fully, we find a direction that heals. Just follow whispers of what sparks compassion in your days once more.

Consider sharing your experience with others coping with hard goodbyes too. Writing down reflections on grief's journey to help comfort hurting souls could inspire healing in them as much as yourself. Journaling your feelings, making bereavement videos online, or joining peer support groups lets your light lift shadows from other lonely paths. Perhaps counseling also brings new perspectives that soothe.

Don't shy away from venturing somewhere entirely new, either, if your spirit is loudly drawing you elsewhere. A fresh start through adventure may be just what's needed to find peace amid change. Moving cities or countries is perfectly alright if it feels right to nurture resilience in new airs and landscapes. You have an explorer's brave heart already, and there's meaning awaiting wherever curiosity leads.

Look for purpose too in simple ways of living well each sunrise despite the darkness that tried stealing purpose away. Your future remains a canvas you can design now, whether pursuing education journeys that excite you and they'd wish for, following wanderlust's pathways to healing, or devoting time to community efforts that bring smiles.

Their legacy lives on through each precious breath you take to experience this rich world, still glowing with hope despite the sorrow that touched your days. Their spirit soars freely within your soul, now inspiring purpose in living joyously, spreading compassion, nurturing growth, and making the most of your gifts. This life is a treasure they ensured could keep flourishing, so walk slowly, love deeply, laugh whenever smiles arise, and let your light radiate as strong as ever, my dear friend.

Take all the time required to rediscover the grandeur of simply being present each sunrise for moments they cannot see. Their memory is honored through embracing the small delights that make this journey worthwhile: spending moments lost in nature's beauty, sharing favorite foods and music with loved ones who stayed, nurturing new dreams however wild they may seem, and helping where you can in any way, big or small.

Have faith that through living fully, finding community, and following whispers of what enriches your heart, purpose will continue to reveal itself beautifully in ways that light your way ahead, one step at a time. You've got this. Their love gives you wings of courage, and now it's time to discover all the places they'll carry your inspiring spirit toward. Your tomorrow remains a gift, so walk steadily and let your resilience write its story through acts of loving kindness where it leads. You were meant for this.

Making It Real

Jordan dragged himself out of bed and slowly got ready for the day. It had been three months since his dad passed away suddenly in a car accident, but the pain still felt as fresh as the day he got the call. He went through the motions of school without really taking anything in, spending every other moment curled up in his room feeling empty.

At first, his friends tried to check on him and offer support, but Jordan rebuffed them all. He couldn't face their sympathy or attempts at distraction; nothing could make this hurt go away.

He just wanted to be left alone with his grief, shutting out the world so no one saw how broken he felt inside.

That Sunday after church let out, Jordan was packing up to leave as quickly as possible when Mr. Troy, the youth pastor, approached him. "Jordan, can I talk to you for a few minutes?" he asked gently. Jordan hesitated, shrugging one shoulder limply as he slumped onto a pew. Part of him wanted to run, but a small part also felt too weary to protest.

Mr. Troy sat beside him quietly for a few moments before speaking. "I know nothing can fill the hole left by losing your dad. The pain of grief feels unbearable at times, like it'll drown you in its waves." Jordan blinked in surprise at how accurately the pastor described what he was going through internally.

"When I lost my best friend in high school, I wanted to shut out the world too," Mr. Troy continued. "But isolating myself only made the hurt grow bigger over time. I had to learn that carrying him with me in my heart and honoring his memory through the little things was better than constantly focusing on missing him."

Jordan frowned. His usual defense was to argue back, but there was kindness and understanding in the pastor's eyes, not judgment, which gave him pause. "What...what do you mean, little things?" he asked hesitantly after a long silence.

Mr. Troy considered it for a moment. "Well, me and my friend Paul used to laugh so much together. So, when I missed him, I started writing down our favorite jokes and funny memories instead of just dwelling on the pain. It helped me remember the joy he brought too."

At that, something inside Jordan shifted as a memory surfaced—dinner table eruptions of laughter from his dad's goofy antics. A small, bitter tear escaped as he replied, "Dad was always making people laugh too. Dinner is so quiet now."

Reaching into his bag, Mr. Troy pulled out a journal and pen, holding them out to Jordan. "Why don't you start writing down some of those jokes and fun times? It might help give your grief a more positive outlet instead of staying stuck in sadness."

Jordan hesitated, his usual rebuttal ready on his lips. But a part of him wanted to cling to those cherished memories rather than let them fade. Wiping his eyes gruffly, he accepted the items with a mumbled, "Thanks." His path ahead stayed clouded, yet a tiny light glimmered at the idea of keeping his dad's silly spirit near.

That week, Jordan started jotting down joke after joke he remembered sharing with his dad across the table. Laughter long gone echoed in his mind as each silly punchline surfaced, bringing a bittersweet smile. Slowly, he began looking forward to that small moment of reflection instead of dreading each new day without answers.

Though sadness still consumed him, Jordan found comfort in those brief moments, keeping his dad's humor, which was so much a part of who he was, alive. Opening up about it to Mr. Troy helped too; he didn't feel so alone bearing the burden anymore. Small pieces of the crushing weight were lifted with each new memory recorded for safekeeping.

More weeks passed, and Jordan began relaying some of the better jokes to Mr. Troy. The pastor's supportive laughter and encouragement gave him the courage to share with trusted friends as well. Though nervous at first, he found solace in their smiles and responses, honoring his dad's spirit too instead of feeling pity.

Before long, what had started as a private healing ritual expanded into something more. Inspired, Jordan started compiling all the jokes, stories, and photos into a small book as a keepsake for loved ones. Poring over old home videos brought on both tears and grins, yet he stayed focused on celebrating cherished times instead of just mourning his dad's absence.

When the book was complete, Jordan was astounded at how full it was—a testament to all the happiness his dad had brought others. Though the ache of loss remained, presenting copies to family and close friends brought fulfillment by seeing them connect to those memories too. His dad's silly ways live on through shared laughter, no longer locked away with just Jordan's grief.

Gradually, the cracks in Jordan's heart began mending from the inside out through this creative outlet. He found purpose in honoring his dad's memory rather than living trapped in pain alone. Dark days still come, as is natural, but each new joke or chuckle brings light, reminding us that grief need not rule the present to remember the love that came before. His dad stays near, not through sadness but through joy instead.

What Am I Supposed to Do Now?

After experiencing such a huge loss, it's easy to feel totally alone and unsure of what to do each day without that beloved person by your side. The future you had imagined is gone, leaving behind only confusion, uncertainty, and an immense ache in your heart that nothing seems to ease. All you want is for this deep pain and sadness to end, but grief has a way of lingering in oceanlike waves that pull you under just when you thought you'd reached calmer waters.

It's so very normal in those first days, weeks, and months after losing someone you love to feel overwhelmed, exhausted, and like you're drifting without an anchor. Perhaps you tend to isolate yourself because sharing your hurt seems impossible or you don't want to burden others. Maybe you're on autopilot but forget things easily and struggle to care for your basic needs because your mind and heart are so wrapped up in grief. However you're experiencing this difficult road, know that each stage is uniquely yours to travel, as gently or turbulently as feels right, without judgment.

One of the most important things as you take those first steps into this new season is to practice self-care and kindness. This means prioritizing extra rest, hydration, nutrition, and self-soothing, which works when emotions feel too turbulent. Allowing yourself to fully feel all the sadness, anger, regret, and other swirling feelings without strict timelines is also key. While crying helps release your emotions, so do comforting baths, walks in nature, journaling, putting on favorite movies, or anything else that nourishes your soul's needs.

Be patient with new priorities emerging each sunrise. While goals seem foreign, focus on one moment at a time rather than work against life's tides. Feel no shame in taking things slower than usual; listen within for wisdom guiding your unique journey after loss's deepest teaching. What served before may not now, and that's alright—honor yourself, adjust your pace, and, by grace, you will show a healing heart. Such treasures often surface through tending grounds within before venturing further afield.

Know that you don't have to walk this winding grief path alone. While periods of quiet are also needed, staying connected to supportive loved ones makes carrying immense sadness less heavy long-term. Don't shy away from relying on others for comfort; they want to offer light where they can't remove the hurt. Speaking with them about your loved one and memories or simply enjoying their reassuring presence nourishes your healing soul when crying comes. Their care reminds us that light remains in a world that has darkened, giving us strength to face each new sunrise.

Using creative outlets is another excellent way to help process the overwhelming grief residing in your heart now. Journaling about memories, feelings, or even songs reminds us to uplift without fully masking turbulent places waves rush toward still. Drawing, photography, music, and other expressive therapies redirect the inward storm outward through talents and gifts, allowing care for the healing self. Small steps outside to release pent-up emotions provides immense relief; don't doubt the power such rituals hold. You deserve comfort, and honest sharing shows immense bravery in getting through dark nights of the soul.

Focusing time and activities on honoring your loved one's memory also gently integrates their bright spirit throughout each new day without them. Perhaps cooking favorite recipes together, looking at photos while listening to shared playlists, volunteering for causes close to their hearts, or simply keeping mementos in a memory box carries them near. Simple daily rituals soften the heaviest hearts over time while lighting pathways ahead, however dim, with qualities beloved in times gone but not forgotten. We are most of what others believe us to be; let their faith guide you ahead too, dear friend.

While grief feels like a shroud covering each moment now, this truth remains: Brighter days steadily rise again for healing hearts to open, receiving life's lessons through difficulties. Even when the sky is cloudy, there is still light to go forward with the faith that the sun is still warming the earth below. Your precious loved one lives on not through absence alone but also through qualities, memories, and love that enrich all those fortunate enough to meet them. Hold fast such gifts, and in time, clinging clouds shall part, revealing horizons ahead where hope and joy once more take wing together with tears shared. Be gentle; keep choosing care for yourself each step.

Conclusion

The journey of grief is long and winding, with many twists and turns along the way. When you first start down that difficult path after losing someone deeply important, it seems impossible that the immense hurt and sadness could ever be lifted. Each day feels dark and heavy as your heart aches from missing that person. You may feel totally alone, wondering how you could possibly find your way through this deep fog of sorrow.

But while grief has no set timeline, I hope this book has shown you that brighter days do steadily rise again with time, care, and allowing your heart to heal at its own pace. The pain will eventually become less sharp, transitioning from a crushing wave that leaves you gasping to a softer memory carried with love instead of anguish. Small steps of self-care, embracing support, creative expression, and honoring cherished memories integrate that beloved spirit gently throughout each new sunrise without them by your side.

Though you still deeply miss who you've lost, their bright lessons of love and life continue guiding your steps even now. They live on through the treasured stories you shared and your continued personal growth as you navigate life's difficulties. With practice over months and years, you learn to look back with more smiles than tears as their memory enriches your journey ahead instead of bringing pain in their absence.

As you walk this rocky valley, grief will gradually shape you into a more empathetic, humble individual who is able to grasp each moment's fleeting beauty. Where darkness taught only sorrow, you will find a new purpose, honoring your loved one's memory through service, creativity, and connection. You can gain strength by walking alongside others also venturing through bereavement's painful yet profoundly meaningful lessons, seeking greater wisdom and compassion. You do not need to travel this trail alone for community lightens what no one can remove, and together your shared light glows brighter.

Though grief feels like a heavy shadow, having faith in love's eternal nature will give you hope to carry on. Your cherished loved one's spirit lives through all they inspired in you and others fortunate to know them—a true legacy whose impacts ripple far beyond their mortal years. Their fingerprints remain on your soul, influencing who you become long after they're gone. And is that not the greatest treasure anyone can leave behind? Long after your loved one is gone, the memories of their compassion and love continue to shape you and inspire those around you. In this way, their influence extends far beyond their time here, creating ripples that touch countless hearts and minds.

Grief's deepest teachings arrive through silence, creative works, humanitarian service, or simply living well with the gratitude each day brings. However your healing soul receives life's difficult yet transformative lessons, know that brighter days will surely come again. Though sadness visits as it must, its visits grow further and further apart with time. And one dawn you will awaken, realizing joy and hope have returned as before, forever changing who you will become and how your relationships will affect this world even long after your final sunset.

For now, have courage, dear friend. Though grief's oceans crash, keep choosing daily comforts for your spirit through trusted people, self-care, creative works, or simply reminiscing from time to time. Your precious loved one lives through all they taught you and continues guiding you forward each new sunrise, however shrouded the skies still remain. Have faith that you will find light again if darkness threatens to overwhelm you. You are not alone on this journey—others walk alongside you with lamps lighting all directions ahead. Your loved one believed in you, so please believe in yourself; have hope and be willing to receive life's bittersweet lessons as they will inevitably give rise to beauty.

About the Author

Juanita Walters is an author whose writing is deeply rooted in compassion, understanding, and a profound appreciation for the resilience of the human spirit. With a background in social work and a specialization in teen grief counselling, Juanita has dedicated her career to supporting teens and young children through some of life's most challenging moments.

Drawing from her experiences as a school counsellor, Juanita brings a unique perspective to teen grief and mental health. She explores the emotional landscapes of adolescence with honesty and empathy, delving into the complexities of grief, loss, and the journey toward a new normal. Through individualization, she offers strategies for teenagers as they navigate the tumultuous terrain of grief and learn to find hope amid despair.

When she's not writing or counselling, Juanita can often be found spending time with her own family, indulging in her love of cooking. She believes in the power of storytelling to inspire empathy, promote healing, and spark meaningful conversations. Juanita is committed to using her voice to make a positive impact in the lives of others. As she continues to explore the human experience through her writing, she invites you to join her on a journey of healing, hope, and resilience.

References

Altru Health System. (2019, August 2). *20 ways to take care of yourself while grieving.* https://www.altru.org/blog/2019/august/20-ways-to-take-care-of-yourself-while-grieving

American Cancer Society. (2020, September 11). *How well are you coping?* https://www.cancer.org/cancer/survivorship/coping/coping-checklist-for-patients.html

Anwar, B. (2023, December 15). *Teen grief 101: How you can help.* Talkspace. https://www.talkspace.com/blog/teen-grief/

Brown, C. (2022, January 26). *How to help a grieving teenager: 10 tips for handling teen grief.* Full Circle. https://fullcirclegc.org/2022/01/26/how-to-help-a-grieving-teenager-10-tips-for-handling-teen-grief/

Clontz, N. (2020, August 27). *How to face a new normal: Adjusting to grief and loss.* Empower Counseling Center. https://empowercounseling.net/how-to-face-a-new-normal-adjusting-to-grief-and-loss/

Dembling, S. (2022, April 22). *Riding the grief roller coaster.* Psychology Today. https://www.psychologytoday.com/intl/blog/widows-walk/202204/riding-the-grief-roller-coaster

Dougy Center. (2020, November 12). *How to help a grieving teen.* https://www.dougy.org/resource-articles/how-to-help-a-grieving-teen

Eluna Network. (n.d.). *Grief by age: High school teens (age 13-18).* https://elunanetwork.org/resources/grief-by-age-high-school-teens-age-13-18

Empathy's Grief Specialists. (n.d.). *Grief triggers.* Empathy. https://www.empathy.com/grief/grief-triggers

Engelman, S. R. (n.d.). *Grieving in your own way: Debunking myths.* https://www.healthpsychologynow.com/grieving-your-own-way.html

Everyone grieves in their own way. (2022, January 8). Caregiver Solutions. https://caregiversolutions.ca/featured-carousel/everyone-grieves-in-their-own-way/

Experiencing grief as a teenager. (n.d.). Vitas Healthcare. https://www.vitas.com/family-and-caregiver-support/grief-and-bereavement/children-and-grief/experiencing-grief-as-a-teenager

Frost, A. (n.d.). *Managing grief: The roller coaster ride.* Attuned Psychology. https://attunedpsychology.com/managing-grief-the-roller-coaster-ride/

Funeral Basics. (2023, November 1). *Coping with grief: What are grief triggers?* https://www.funeralbasics.org/coping-grief-triggers/

Grief. (2019). KidsHealth. https://kidshealth.org/en/teens/someone-died.html

Healthwise Staff. (2023, March 7). *Grief: Helping teens with grief.* Health Link BC. https://www.healthlinkbc.ca/pregnancy-parenting/relationships-and-emotional-health/grief-helping-teens-grief

Integrative Life Center. (2020, October 29). *Grief and loss: How to accept death.* https://integrativelifecenter.com/mental-health-treatment/grief-and-loss-how-to-accept-death/

Meadows-Fernandez, A. R. (2017, May 25). *6 healthy ways I've learned to accept death.* Healthline. https://www.healthline.com/health/grief-without-denial-6-healthy-ways-to-accept-death

Milano, A. (2022, November 8). *Strategies to handle unexpected grief triggers after the loss of a loved one.* Milano Monuments. https://www.milanomonuments.com/blog/strategies-to-handle-unexpected-grief-triggers-after-the-loss-of-a-loved-one

Oates, J. R., & Maani-Fogelman, P. A. (2022). *Nursing grief and loss.* StatPearls Publishing. https://www.ncbi.nlm.nih.gov/books/NBK518989/

Presutti, L. (2023, June 6). *Dealing with grief triggers: Understanding and managing reminders of loss.* River Oaks Psychology. https://riveroakspsychology.com/dealing-with-grief-triggers-understanding-and-managing-reminders-of-loss/

Royden, L. (2018, December 6). *A new normal.* Psychology Today. https://www.psychologytoday.com/us/blog/the-mourning-after/201812/new-normal

Smith, C. (2021, October 1). *Recognizing grief trigger warnings.* Psychology Today. https://www.psychologytoday.com/us/blog/writing-between-the-lines/202110/recognizing-grief-trigger-warnings

Stanaway, C. (2020, June 8). *The stages of grief: Accepting the unacceptable.* University of Washington.

https://wellbeing.uw.edu/the-stages-of-grief-accepting-the-unacceptable/

Swanson, D. (2023, July 25). *Grief is an emotional roller coaster.* Hope for Widows Foundation. https://hopeforwidows.org/2023/07/grief-is-an-emotional-roller-coaster/

Vickers, M. (n.d.). *Teen grief 101: Helping a teenager deal with loss.* Eterneva. https://www.eterneva.com/resources/teenager-grief

Winston's Wish. (2020, April 14). *Do children grieve differently to adults?* \https://www.winstonswish.org/do-children-grieve-differently/

Wolfelt, A. D. (2023, December 21). *Helping teenagers cope with grief.* Center for Loss & Life Transition. https://www.centerforloss.com/2023/12/helping-teenagers-cope-grief/

Made in the USA
Monee, IL
26 March 2025

14717256R00066